What would
Jesus say 2:

What would Jesus say 2:

David Beckham | Big Brother Eminem | Harry Potter
Philip Pullman | Paula Radcliffe | Anne Robinson
Homer Simpson | Robbie Williams | YOU ?

Steve Ayers

Inter-Varsity Press

INTER-VARSITY PRESS
38 De Montfort Street, Leicester LE1 7GP, England
Email: ivp@uccf.org.uk
Website: www.ivpbooks.com

First published 2003

British Library Cataloguing in Publication Data
A catalogue record for this book is available from the British Library.

ISBN 0–85111–799–6

Set in Dante 10.5/13pt
Typeset in Great Britain by CRB Associates, Reepham, Norfolk
Printed and bound in Great Britain by Creative Print and Design (Wales), Ebbw Vale

Inter-Varsity Press is the publishing division of the Universities and Colleges Christian Fellowship (formerly the Inter-Varsity Fellowship), a student movement linking Christian Unions in universities and colleges throughout Great Britain, and a member movement of the International Fellowship of Evangelical Students. For more information about local and national activities write to UCCF, 38 De Montfort Street, Leicester LE1 7GP, email us at email@uccf.org.uk, or visit the UCCF website at www.uccf.org.uk.

Contents

Preface

Even something as solitary as writing a book is a team effort, or at least that's the way I prefer to do it. I got a lot of encouragement from different people and I'm grateful for all their help.

Cherianne, Phil, Liz, Geoff, and Linda read the drafts and were very encouraging, as well as pointing out all the things I needed to rewrite. They told me very gently and I do appreciate it.

Stephanie Heald is a great editor and her input made this book much better than it would have been otherwise. Writing *WWJS2* also made me realize what a great job Jason Lane did in the first one.

Linda, Becky and Ben were stars; thanks for everything. I had a lot of other good people praying for me too; thank you.

Finally, Catherine was a great encouragement to me with her input, and she spurred me on to the end. This book is for her.

Steve Ayers

Introduction

Fame, Fame, fatal Fame
it can play hideous tricks on the brain
but still I'd rather be Famous
than righteous or holy, any day.
Morrissey, 'Frankly, Mr Shankley'

We live in peculiar times. We seem to be ever in the thrall of celebrities. We live in an age of idols and, with ever more media outlets offering ever more space to be filled, the demand for details about the way that celebrities work, rest and (particularly) play seems to go on for ever. There are column inches and celebrity magazines to fill each week. We live in a world of celebrity chefs, celebrity gardeners and even celebrity decorators, for heaven's sake. If these things don't strike you as being the teensiest bit strange it's because you've forgotten (or not known) a world before them.

The desire to be famous seems to drive so many of us. Millions of us labour under the delusion that it's somehow unjust that we still haven't been discovered. We may be in an accounts office or waiting on tables at the moment, but sooner or later we'll be discovered and able to take our rightful place as a *bona fide* celebrity. People will recognize us for the true talents that we are; we shall be applauded by appreciative crowds. As the old song quoted above implies, why would anyone want to be a hero of any moral substance when they could be famous? So it's off to that *PopIdolBigBrotherSurvivor* audition and the possibility of a lot more than fifteen minutes of fame. These days, with all the time to be filled by the digital channels, we should be good for fifteen hours or even fifteen days.

Who doesn't want to be a millionaire? Who doesn't want to be famous? There aren't many who don't, which might not be too surprising. But as we step back from the dream we realize that we are actually talking hardcore fantasy here. Fame and riches for all? It can't be. After all, someone has to sit on the pavement applauding as the parade goes past.

Fame is a fickle creature. Just four years ago Jason Lane and I wrote what turned out to be the first volume of *What Would Jesus Say to ...?* We looked at some of the biggest celebrities around and tried to work out what Jesus would have to say about the situation they found themselves in.

As our culture hurtles ever onwards, some of the people who were big then are beginning to fade from the memory a little. Four years is a long time in the fame game. So I've looked at some new people, people who weren't such big news four years ago, or who weren't household names then. In each case I've taken words from the Bible that seem particularly relevant to their lives, convinced as I am that the Bible is unique in the extent to which it reads us as we read it.

These, then, are the latest crop of celebrities. You'd better read on, quick, because a pound to a penny half of this lot won't be around with anything like the same high profile in a few years' time. There will be someone or something new to take their places. In the coming years some of the current crop might become more famous, but most will have faded. The careers of others will defy prediction; who would have thought that Ozzy Osbourne, once the reviled frontman with Black Sabbath, would become the star of his own soap opera and perform for the Queen? It's a strange world!

Finally, it is, of course, the greatest irony that the most famous and the least fashionable person in this book is going to outlast anything that any of the celebrities here (or you and I) ever do or achieve.

What would Jesus have to say to Homer Simpson, Eminem, Paula Radcliffe and the rest? Some of the answers might be surprising. Jesus was constantly surprising the people around him. To answer the question 'What would Jesus say to . . . ?' I've looked at the way Jesus spoke to people two thousand years ago and the way issues are addressed in the Bible, a much better bet than making it up myself. If you have any doubts, check out the life of Jesus as recorded in one of the Gospel accounts written by those who were with them. Prepare to be surprised!

At the end of the book we'll take some time out to consider what Jesus might say to us – you and me; Joe and Joanne Public – because Jesus would talk to anyone, and in fact spent the vast majority of his time with nonentities like us. Although he spent time with the great and good, not to mention the simply notorious, one of the marks of Jesus is that he had time for everyone. I, for one, am very glad of that.

Let's start with someone whose encounter with Jesus you'd pay good money to listen to. What would Jesus say to Philip Pullman?

What would Jesus say 2:
Philip Pullman?

Melvyn Bragg: 'So she [Eve] was right to eat the apple?'
Philip Pullman: 'Absolutely. Bang on. Good for her.'[1]

'Who?!'

Once upon a time at a certain football ground there was tradition among the crowd when the opposition put on a substitute. The home supporters would noisily 'Sssh!' each other as the announcer gave the details of the substitution over the tannoy. When the substitute's name was announced the crowd would cry, 'Who?!' in unison, presumably destroying any confidence the poor substitute had to start with.

A few people picking up this book might have a similar feeling. Here's a book on Jesus and famous people, and we're starting with Philip Pullman, who might be the least familiar of all the names featured in this book. While some names (Beckham, Eminem, Harry Potter) are globally recognized, Pullman is, at least at the time of writing, less well known. Even if I were to tell you that he is a children's author, you might be none the wiser. Yet he is an important writer, addressing the big questions of life while apparently writing for nine-to-twelve-year-olds.

Like J. K. Rowling, Pullman (though he's no fan of Harry Potter) appeals to readers of every age. He has been writing for many years since leaving the teaching profession, but has come to prominence through *His Dark Materials*, a trilogy that saw him win a number of prizes and become the first children's author to win the prestigious Whitbread Award with the third book, *The Amber Spyglass*, in 2001. Even if you haven't heard of him yet, you will. October 2003 saw the publication of *Lyra's Oxford*, a short story set in the same world as *His Dark Materials*, and at Christmas the National Theatre made the interesting choice to stage the trilogy as their seasonal offering. We can also look forward to the movie, with Tom Stoppard writing the screenplay for the company that produced *The Lord of the Rings*. Pullman's writings are set to become a major influence. Certainly Russell T. Davies's drama *The Second Coming*, in which the Son of God returns to perform a miracle at Manchester City's Maine Road stadium (and how they need one!), was heavily influenced by the books. Both works come to the same conclusion: essentially that, if there was no religion, the world would be a better place, as we might work harder at creating a paradise on earth.

Indeed, Pullman has a great sense of wonder about the planet we live on, and has something to teach those Christians who misguidedly believe that the world is such a terrible and corrupt place that they must shun everything it has to offer. As he sees it, 'This [the world we live in] is all there is; and it is extremely beautiful and full of the most exquisite delight. That's what I mean about the republic of heaven. It's already around us. I just wanted to make that a bit more explicit, to give it a name.'[2]

While Christians cannot agree with the first part of his statement, we agree that the world, even after the way that we have mistreated it, is an amazing place. We would expect that to be the case, given a belief in the way that God designed it. Presumably Pullman sees it as a happy accident.

His enthusiasm for the planet he lives on was fired by a childhood in which he saw a lot of the world, living in Rhodesia and Australia in his formative years, as well as in various locations in Britain. When he was just seven his father, an RAF pilot, died during the Mau Mau rising in Kenya, which resulted in his living for a time with his clergyman grandfather in Norfolk. It's an episode that has led to speculation about the childhood he enjoyed there, given his later antipathy to the church, although in interviews he insists it was a happy time.

His Dark Materials is staggering in the ground that it covers. Although Pullman describes the story as being about 'the difference between children and adults',[3] there is a lot more to the books than that. Issues addressed include the big questions of life. Where do we go when we die? What is God like? *Is* there a God? Are there worlds other than our own? What are the qualities in life that we should admire? What importance do we place on wisdom? What, if any, is the place of the church? All this, don't forget, in a children's book.

> I can't stand fantasy novels. Show me a mythical quest and a talking bear, and I'm first out of the door. But this book ... I was reading one of the closing chapters [of *The Amber Spyglass*] on a train; I was crying so much, the ticket inspector asked me if I needed help.
>
> *Russell T. Davies, playwright*

As well as the scope of the books, the imagination that they display is amazing. We have wheeled beasts and a knife that cuts through into new universes. There is an alethiometer, which always tells the truth about any situation and is able to predict the future. We're introduced to miniature Gallipean spies. Rather wonderfully, there are armoured polar bears too, and, most famously, daemons. These are the animals that go everywhere with you and represent something of your nature. What precisely are they? Guardian angels? Externalized souls? Conscience? It's hard to pin down exactly, though there is surely something in each of these. Whatever they are, Pullman draws on Greek legend and traditional southern American shamanism and gives them an inventive twist.

In an age where so much adult writing is consumed with the trivia of our age, it seems that these books are asking the big questions that we dare not tackle once our daemons settle into their fixed form. The reception of the novels has not been without controversy, although surprisingly they have attracted less criticism than Harry Potter. As Pullman admits, he was happy to sneak in on the back of J. K. Rowling's books. Nevertheless, some, such as Peter Hitchens, have been vocal in their criticism. Hitchens sees the books as a deliberate reversal of C. S. Lewis's Narnia Chronicles (again, don't mention them to Pullman; he hates them), and rather amusingly Hitchens describes the author as the 'Anti-Lewis'.

Pullman certainly likes to be provocative, portraying the church as a thoroughly cruel and wicked institution, and writing of male angels in love. (He claims not to know if they are gay or not, though the majority would read the story that way.) He rewrites the story of Adam and Eve and cheers when they eat the fruit, and then for good measure he kills off the Ancient of Days.

What would Jesus say to Philip Pullman? For someone so adamant in his opposition to God and the church, it would certainly make for an interesting encounter! Yet Philip Pullman *might* have time for Jesus. His attitude to Christ comes across as a little confused and muddled, although I don't criticize him for that; on this issue he's hardly unusual.

On the one hand he speaks to Melvyn Bragg (on *The South Bank Show*) about Jesus in glowing if unconventional terms. Asked in the interview about Jesus Christ and 'the wonderful things of the church', Pullman replied, 'If only people listened to Jesus instead of the priests that came after him we'd all be a lot better off.'

So perhaps Philip Pullman would take the time and effort to listen to Jesus. I dare say there would be times when he felt compelled to disagree with Jesus. In an interview with *Third Way* magazine he was quick to dismiss Jesus' statement that 'Unless you become like children, you will never enter the kingdom of heaven' with the comment, 'He wasn't right all the time.'[4] Later in *The South Bank Show* interview he talks about his view that Jesus was directly inspired by the rebel angels, hence the words of wisdom that he spoke. He proffers the view that, because of the truth of Jesus' teaching, it has been denied and painted over by the church authorities that followed him.

As I say, it's a cloudy picture, but he's hardly the first person to have trouble working out who Jesus is. Some of us have had help to think it through by examining Jesus' words for ourselves, while others are still trying to figure it out.

What would Jesus say about how we become wise?

With so many topics to choose from, where would Jesus start? It could be a wide-ranging conversation. Pullman, the man of whom *The Observer* asked, 'Is he the best storyteller ever?', would meet Jesus, who must be in with a shout on that score himself. Perhaps first of all Jesus might talk to Pullman about how we become wise. It's a big theme for the author, who, like many of the people Jesus met, seems to be a truth-seeker, someone who is more interested than most in finding out what the world is truly about. Jesus always took time to sit and talk with anyone who was serious about discovering the truth. So, if Philip Pullman or any of us were to approach Jesus about how we get to be wise, Jesus would be sure to talk about it. To understand Pullman's view of how we get wise we need to look at what he does with one of the oldest stories in the Bible.

In his retelling of the story of Adam and Eve, Pullman comes up with a viewpoint very different from that of the Bible. As he explains to Melvyn Bragg, he sees the story as being about 'the important and inevitable process of developing as human beings. We have to go through this stage of discovery, rebellion, estrangement, self-consciousness, in order to become wise. Unless we do that we can't become wise. We get stuck in a sort of childhood.'

When Bragg asks, 'So she was right to eat the apple?', Pullman doesn't hesitate to confirm, 'Absolutely. Bang on. Good for her.' In an earlier interview Pullman goes even further, explaining that 'sin, or what churches have called sin, is in fact a very important stage in human development'.[5]

In other words, it is only in disobeying God that we begin to grow and develop as human beings. While the story of Adam and Eve's disobedience in the Bible (which we look at in the chapter on *Big Brother*) sees that disobedience to God as a terrible thing resulting in separation from God, Pullman sees it as a good thing.

Because he believes that Adam and Eve's disobedience brought about a new consciousness that enables us to search for wisdom and become wise, he applauds them. Indeed, 'Satan in this scenario "is understood to be good rather than evil". In the Biblical story (Genesis 3), Satan was instrumental in bringing about what Pullman calls "the best thing, the most important thing that ever happened to us, and if we had our heads on straight on this issue, we would have churches dedicated to Eve instead of the Virgin Mary." '[6]

So, Jesus might start by talking to Philip Pullman about where you go in the search to become wise. It's something that most of us want in life, to be a bit (or a lot!) wiser. How do we go about that search? Philip Pullman says that the beginning of wisdom is to throw off the shackles of religion and to stride out bravely to discover wisdom for ourselves.

Jesus would disagree.

While neither Jesus or Pullman is a fan of dry religion, they would have very different ideas about the way wisdom is attained. For Pullman it's a question of cutting loose and discovering things for ourselves, an attractive proposition in our independent-minded society. By way of contrast, Jesus makes what seems, on the face of it, an incredibly arrogant claim. As with many of his dangerous claims, it's smuggled in as an apparently harmless story:

> Anyone who listens to my teaching and obeys me is wise, like a person
> who builds a house on solid rock. Though the rain comes in torrents

and the floodwaters rise and the winds beat against that house, it won't collapse, because it is built on rock. But anyone who hears my teaching and ignores it is foolish, like a person who builds a house on sand. When the rains and floods come and the winds beat against that house, it will fall with a mighty crash.[7]

We might know this story quite well and still miss the force of what Jesus is saying here. The essence of the story is this. If you want to be wise you need to listen to Jesus and act upon what he teaches. To do so is to build a firm foundation for your life, whereas those who listen to Jesus and don't do anything about it are like those people who figure it's great down on the beach and so they build on the sand. Which is all very well until the weather forecast starts looking a bit dicey. When that happens you're in serious trouble.

So it might well be that the first thing Jesus would talk to Philip Pullman about would be how you get to be wise. It's not by striking out on your own but by listening to what Jesus is saying.

What would Jesus say God is like?

He must be so old – I've never seen anyone suffering like that …
Lyra on her encounter with God[8]

Alternatively, Jesus might speak to Pullman about what God is like. It's one of the major questions of Pullman's trilogy, as well as being a fundamental question that has exercised the minds of many of us, throughout the ages and across the world. What would Jesus say to Philip Pullman about God?

The way Pullman describes God is very different from the Christian understanding of him. For a start, Pullman's version of God is an angel who cheated his way to prominence, falsely claiming to be the Creator. As the one of the rebel angels explains:

> The Authority, God, the Creator, the Lord, Yahweh, El, Adonai, the King, the Father, the Almighty – these are all names he gave himself. He was never the creator. He was an angel – the first angel, true, the most powerful, but he was formed of Dust as we are ... He told those who came after him that he had created them, but it was a lie. One of those who came later was wiser than he was, and she found out the truth, so he banished her. We serve her still.[9]

He's also getting on a bit. As time has unfolded, God has become older and more feeble until, at the end his life, the Authority is painted as tired, powerless and pathetic.

> ... he was so old, and he was terrified, crying like a baby and cowering away into the lowest corner ... Demented and powerless, the aged being could only weep and mumble in fear and pain and misery ...[10]

Although few have dared to paint it quite so vividly, you could argue that it's quite a popular portrait of God. If many of us were to take the time to articulate how we thought of God, maybe we'd be honest enough to admit that we don't see too much evidence of his being as powerful as is always being claimed for him. Even if the way Pullman sees God is a little overdrawn, perhaps it has crossed your mind either that God is absent or that the whole thing is way out of his control these days.

> It's a minority religion. It's beleaguered – it's no kind of threat.
> *Journalist Polly Toynbee on Christianity*[11]

Pullman, a supporter of the British Humanist Association and an Honorary Associate of the National Secular Society, says that he sees no evidence for the existence of any God. By his own description he hovers somewhere between atheist and agnostic, and declares, 'I've got no evidence whatever for believing in a God. But I know that all the things I do know are very small compared with the things that I don't know. So maybe there is a

God out there. All I know is that if there is, he hasn't shown himself on earth.'[12]

In *His Dark Materials*, where there is a God, the Authority is so fragile that being exposed to the wind is too much for him. As he is finally put out of his misery he seems to be relieved to die. The death is recorded briefly and without any great sense of importance, underlining the insignificance that he seems to have for Pullman in life as well as in his story.

God looks very different in the Gospels, which record the life of Jesus. There is a wealth of material that contradicts Pullman's portrait of God. There are so many incidents we could look at in thinking about what we know of God from Jesus. I'll look at just one, and you can read a whole host of others if you look at the life of Jesus for yourself.

Early in Mark's biography, Jesus is besieged by people who want to come and hear him and perhaps get healed too:

Several days later Jesus returned to Capernaum, and the news of his arrival spread quickly through the town. Soon the house where he was staying was so packed with visitors that there wasn't room for one more person, not even outside the door. And he preached the word to them. Four men arrived carrying a paralyzed man on a mat. They couldn't get to Jesus through the crowd, so they dug through the clay roof above his head. Then they lowered the sick man on his mat, right down in front of Jesus.[13]

You can imagine the commotion! The place was packed, and if you were lucky enough to secure a place inside the house you might find yourself showered with bits of debris as these friends of the paralysed man start to tear a hole in the roof and come in through the ceiling.

Can you imagine what it must have been like for this man to be lowered down in full view of everyone too? It's some entrance; this is not for the faint-hearted. And as he was lowered down by his friends he must, at some stage, have been at eye-level with

Jesus. Now what? 'Seeing their faith, Jesus said to the paralyzed man, "My son, your sins are forgiven." ' [14]

Forgive me for saying this, but I'm not sure that the guy would have been all that pleased at this outcome. His friends had gone to extraordinary lengths to get this man to Jesus. He wanted to meet with Jesus – for what reason? To get his sins forgiven? Hardly! The man wanted to be healed! You can imagine him thinking, 'What do you mean, my sins are forgiven? Forget that – I want to walk!'

Some of the religious establishment got very agitated at this because they weren't best pleased. 'But some of the teachers of religious law who were sitting there said to themselves, "What? This is blasphemy! Who but God can forgive sins!" ' [15]

What they saw clearly, and what we don't realize as readily, is that in this act Jesus was taking on something that only God can do. By forgiving the man his sins, Jesus was staking a massive claim. This claim to be able to forgive sins was a claim to be much more than another religious teacher or maker of miracles. He was claiming to be able to do what only God can do. To back up such an outrageous claim he then told them, 'Just so that you know I'm able to do this, I'll heal him too.'

> Jesus knew what they were discussing among themselves, so he said to them, 'Why do you think this is blasphemy? Is it easier to say to the paralyzed man, "Your sins are forgiven" or "Get up, pick up your mat, and walk"? I will prove that I, the Son of Man, have the authority on earth to forgive sins.' Then Jesus turned to the paralyzed man and said, 'Stand up, take your mat, and go on home, because you are healed!' The man jumped up, took the mat, and pushed his way through the stunned onlookers. Then they all praised God. 'We've never seen anything like this before!' they exclaimed. [16]

In contrast to the scared, feeble, uninterested, powerless, rheumy-eyed creature of Pullman's tale, we have Jesus. He's often described as the Son of God, and he tells his closest followers that if they've seen him they've seen the Father. [17] In other words, Jesus was God in the flesh, living among his people. He revealed a God who is passionately involved with his people, even stepping into his creation in order to rescue us, putting our lives back together, reconciling us with himself as he grieves over our waywardness. He's all the things that Pullman's dismal vision of God isn't, and there's no way of reconciling the two views. It would make for a fascinating conversation if Jesus were to talk to Philip Pullman about what God is like. As for any of us, it's hardly a fair fight. How can we be expected to win an argument with God about what he's like?

What would Jesus say about what happens when we die?

The fundamental thing behind all motivation and all activity is the constant struggle against annihilation and against death. It's absolutely stupefying in its terror, and it renders anyone's accomplishments meaningless.[18]

Woody Allen

Similarly, it's an ambitious man who would want to argue with Jesus about what happens when we die. Most people with whom we could debate this don't have a lot of first-hand experience of the subject matter. Jesus is rather better versed on the topic than others! The events of Easter gave him a unique insight into death and its power, or rather its lack of power. Death and what happens when we die is another of those big topics that Pullman tackles in *His Dark Materials*, so what would Jesus say to Philip Pullman about death?

From early in the tale the stated ambition of Lord Asriel is to defeat death. As he tells Lyra in the first part of the trilogy, 'Somewhere out there is the origin of all the Dust, all the death, the sin, the misery, the destructiveness in the world. Human beings can't see anything without wanting to destroy it, Lyra. *That's* original sin. And I'm going to destroy it. Death is going to die.'[19]

'Death is going to die.' It's a phrase that could almost have come out of the Bible. They are similar to the words Paul wrote to the church in Corinth, except that he tells us that death has already died – past tense – because Jesus went and beat it when he rose from death.

> Death is swallowed up in victory. O death, where is your victory? O death, where is your sting? ...
>
> How we thank God, who gives us victory over sin and death through Jesus Christ our Lord![20]

Jesus rose from the dead. You can read about it in all four accounts of his life – Matthew, Mark, Luke and John – and I'd strongly recommend that you do. By dying the way he did on a cross on a hill in first-century Jerusalem he defeated death and sin (the things that separate us from God). We'll look at this in more detail in later chapters, but, for now, know that this is a crucial part of the Christian message. A little earlier in that letter to the Corinthians Paul argued with those in the early church who were claiming that there was no resurrection of the dead. He gathered all his chips and staked everything that he had lived and worked for on this: that Christ had been raised from the dead.

> ... if Christ has not been raised, our preaching is useless and so is your faith. More than that, we are then found to be false witnesses about God, for we have testified about God that he raised Christ from the dead. But he did not raise him if in fact the dead are not raised. For if the dead are not raised, then Christ has not been raised either. And if Christ has not been raised, your faith is futile; you are still in your sins. Then those also who have fallen asleep in Christ are lost. If only for this life we have hope in Christ, we are to be pitied more than all men.
>
> But Christ has indeed been raised from the dead ...[21]

Bold words! If there's no bodily, physical, resurrection there's no faith. No hope. Full stop. The message that Paul preached is useless. So is any faith anyone is stupid enough to place in that message. Your faith is futile; you're still dead in your sins – if there is no resurrection. We're pitiful if we figure that Christianity is something nice for now but that there is no heaven. 'But Christ', asserts Paul, 'has indeed been raised from the dead.' The life, death and resurrection of Jesus make the bold claim that death is not the end, and that there is something beyond death.

If death is not the end, what happens when we die? When Will asks this question in *The Amber Spyglass*, the rebel angels tell him of the world of the dead, a 'prison camp' set up by the Authority. What happens there? ' "It's impossible to say," said Baruch. "Everything about it is secret. Even the churches don't know; they tell their believers that they'll live in Heaven, but that's a lie." ' [22]

Lyra and Will make their way to the world of the dead.

> They found themselves on a great plain that extended far ahead into the mist ... Standing on the floor of this huge space were adults and children – ghost-people – so many that Lyra couldn't guess their number. At least, most of them were standing, though some were sitting and some lying down listless or asleep. No one was moving about, or running or playing, though many of them turned to look at these new arrivals, with a fearful curiosity in their wide eyes. [23]

It's a bleak vision of life after death, which maybe owes something to Dante in its composition. It's grey and desolate, bereft of hope or light, a place where Harpies terrorize the dead with screams for all of eternity.

Eventually Lyra and Will manage to free those trapped in the world of the dead. They offer them a way out, not in a physical resurrection but in dissolving into the world from which they came, so that 'we'll be alive again in a thousand blades of grass, and a million leaves, we'll be falling in the raindrops and blowing in the fresh breeze, we'll be glittering in the dew under the stars and the moon out there in the physical world which is our true home and always was.' [24]

It's a very different version of the afterlife from the one that Jesus speaks of. As the time draws near when he is about to go to the cross, Jesus reassures his disciples:

'Don't be troubled. You trust God, now trust in me. There are many rooms in my Father's home, and I am going to prepare a place for you. If this were not so, I would tell you plainly. When everything is ready, I will come and get you, so that you will always be with me where I am.'[25]

As we'll see when we look at what Jesus would have to say to Homer Simpson, heaven is described as a wedding feast, a party where there's a great celebration. Jesus promises that he's gone on ahead to prepare a place for those who love and trust him. We'll talk more about this later, but for now we'll simply acknowledge that Pullman and Jesus disagree about heaven. Pullman doesn't believe in it at all. As far as he's concerned, when you die that's it; nothing beyond the grave. Hence his enthusiasm for making the most of this life.

What would Jesus have to say about us?

Finally, what would Jesus say to Philip Pullman about human beings? In particular, is it possible to create heaven on earth in the way the author dreams? It's one thing to want to kill off death. It's quite another to decide to kill off the Almighty. It is, of course, very convenient to kill off God. That way we figure we can start again with a clean slate and, even better, we can start living by the rules that we make up. We are no longer in bondage to the laws God imposes upon us; we are now free to decide for ourselves how to live. A result of all this? We get to judge what is good and what is evil, no longer bound by the arbitrary and ancient rules of religion. Liberated from all that, we are able to start afresh, each taking responsibility for establishing a republic of heaven, heaven on earth.

As Pullman acknowledges, heaven exerts a powerful pull on us. Explaining this on *The South Bank Show* he says:

Heaven embodies a lot of ideas that are important to all of us, principally the idea of meaningfulness. The idea that our lives are not meaningless ... the sense that we are connected to one another, that we are connected to the wider universe ... is a very important one to us. It's very hard to give up, it's very hard to live without it. When we come to realize that God is dead or that he never existed, do we have to give up the kingdom? Well, we have to give up the kingdom because there's no King. But I don't think we have to give up heaven. If there isn't a kingdom of heaven there needs to be a republic of heaven, a republic where we are all equal and valuable citizens and not subjects. And there isn't a priesthood on high and the rest of us below; we're all equal citizens, with an equal responsibility; that follows from that.[26]

To Pullman it's vital that the church, with its priesthood, should have no part in the republic of heaven. He has a very dim view of institutionalized religion and of priests, pastors and ministers. In his book the priests are, without exception, all drinkers, zealots, cruel or mean, with daemons to match. What lies behind this is his assertion that

Churches of every sort and of every religion have got hold of a very good way of controlling human lives, for reasons that are ultimately selfish and cruel. They borrow an authority from a non-existent God or being and wield power over human lives ... Wherever you look throughout the world you find religious authorities, specifically churches of one sort or another, specifically priests, wielding authority and telling people not to do things, and punishing them furiously and savagely if they disobey.[27]

When they see what I am saying; that yes, churches are bad, sin, or what churches have called sin, is in fact a very important stage in human development, there may be some objections. I hope so.[28]

Philip Pullman

Pullman's portrayal of the church as an evil and cruel institution is obviously ridiculous and lop-sided (and perhaps the dictates of children's literature demand this). Of course, there have been examples of tremendous cruelty done in the name of religion. Just outside the walls of the city where I live there is a monument to men and women who were put to death for their Protestant faith. Catholics, Jews, Muslims, witches and others have all been persecuted in different times and places, some tortured and killed by groups that didn't agree with them on matters of faith. I don't know of a single Christian who would say that the cruelty inflicted on people in these situations was a good thing. Some of the acts done in the name of religion (and some of those that had nothing to do with faith at all) were clearly awful.

But what about all the good things that came about due to the diligence and dedication of men and women who found their inspiration from loving Christ? What about those who set up hospitals and universities, schools and housing schemes, soup runs and shelters, hospices and orphanages, even the trade-union movement? I'm not suggesting that you have to be a Christian to be involved in any of these fields, but history tells us that the men and women who pioneered in these areas and many others were very often motivated to do so by a strong Christian conviction. Having experienced and been changed by the love of Christ, many men and women have gone on to dedicate their lives to showing something of that love to those around them. The people of the church are not the evil empire that Pullman paints them. As Sarah Johnson commented in *The Times*, there must be a danger 'that young readers will take Pullman's "Church" for the real thing, and many will be so drawn in by the power of the narrative that they will never again be able "to explore faith without a Pullmanesque bias". Such a situation would be an utter tragedy.'[29]

The other side of this particular coin is that Pullman's utopian dream is destined to go the same way as all such attempts by any human agency to establish heaven on earth. Whether motivated by political, religious or atheist ideology, any attempt to legislate for the kingdom on earth is surely doomed. Philip Pullman, despite his protestations that he knows what children are like and that therefore he doesn't idolize them, has a ridiculously high opinion of human beings. He seems to think that, if we can all find a way to pull together, we'll somehow be able to put things right. And yet, as other literature from *Lord of The Flies* to *The Beach* has spelt out for us, and as we've surely observed from having our eyes open as we look around us, it's going to take a great deal more than 'trying a bit harder' on the part of the human race. It might be possible to improve things a little, or for a while, if we all work hard and try our best to live in harmony with one another. But our seemingly endless appetite for selfishness and sin will always wreck any chance we have to create heaven on earth, even within the church. It's a nice theory, but heaven on earth takes more faith than most of us can muster.

So, as you can see, there's plenty that Jesus might talk to Philip Pullman about. How receptive Pullman might be to such a conversation is another matter. I think he might look forward to the argument, though it's debatable how interested he might be in considering the possibility that he might be wrong. Again, he's hardly unusual in that. At least Pullman has given some thought to these matters, even if, sadly, his opinion is reflected in the words of Mary Malone towards the end of the trilogy: 'I saw that there wasn't any God at all and that physics was more interesting anyway. The Christian religion is a very powerful and convincing mistake, that's all.' [30]

Is Mary Malone right? Is physics more interesting than *anything*? More seriously, is Christianity simply a very powerful and convincing mistake? The rest of this book will be exploring that question. First of all we'll think about this question of human nature. It might seem strange to turn to a TV game show to consider further what we are like as human beings. Yet even when people are on their better behaviour in front of the TV cameras, as with shows like *Big Brother*, we see a more realistic and perhaps a more depressing version of the human race than that dreamt of by Philip Pullman.

2

What would Jesus say 2:
Big Brother?

From Jade to jaded

Jade Goody was a tabloid editor's dream. Hailing from a humble background, her dad has been in and out of prison and her mum is a one-armed lesbian. It doesn't get much better than that, does it? With that and her antics in the house, Jade was on the front pages of one or other of the tabloid papers fifty-two times over the summer of 2002, all this despite the fact that the World Cup Finals were on. Much of Jade's coverage was less than complimentary.

When she was finally evicted, she was greeted with a congratulatory message from Johnny Depp, an invitation to appear on Graham Norton's show, and a cheque for £250,000 or £500,000 (depending on who you believe) from News International for her story and a week of her time.

We've come a long way. In 1948 Eric Blair (better known as George Orwell) wrote a book about the future in which people are all subjects in a totalitarian state. Central to *Nineteen Eighty-Four* are the television sets that are used to monitor what is going on in the homes of everyone. Placards in the street proclaim that 'Big Brother is watching you'. Well, in a twist that George Orwell would have been hard pushed to imagine, at the start of the third millennium the tables were turned. We watched *Big Brother*.

We've come a long way, but is it progress? As Reality TV took hold of the schedules (along with either Davina MacColl or Ant and Dec) we watched people aiming to survive tough ordeals, their efforts to achieve stardom and their everyday work life. C-list celebrities toughed it out in the jungle before, in some cases, begging, 'Get me out of here!' We were even treated to *Celebrity Detox Camp* as well as films such as *The Truman Show* and *EdTV*. Everywhere, it seems, we were watching other people.

Perhaps biggest and best, though (if such a thing could be claimed), is *Big Brother*. Versions were made around the world, and despite the fears (or hopes, depending on your view of the show) that it would be a flash in the pan, the show just grew. The third series was more successful than the previous two, with the final night attracting 9.9 million viewers. Not only was this the largest audience Channel Four had ever attracted, but for the first time it drew a greater overall audience share than any of its rivals for that day.

Did you see it? Were you addicted to it? Did you wait up to watch it, only to wonder, after spending half an hour watching a group of people looking very bored, why? Did you go one stage further? Unable to wait for the highlights, did you watch the uninterrupted footage on satellite television? I know of one insomniac who sat up watching the residents in the house as they slept. I'm also told that the show is good to iron to, perhaps if only because ironing suddenly seems relatively interesting. Certainly there was a time during the second celebrity edition when I realized I was watching Les Dennis and his new friends looking for a spanner. What was I doing!?

In case, by some strange quirk of fate, you managed to miss the daily shows over each ten-week run, I should give you a quick run-down of what it's all about. The basic premise is that ten or twelve people (the format changes from time to time) stay in a house together for twenty-four hours a day. Every week each of the contestants has to nominate the two people they would like to leave the house. These nominations are added up, and the top two, or, in the event of a tie, three or four people, are then voted for by the viewers in a phone poll.

It does seem that the *Big Brother* format has run its course now, though, the fourth series having plumbed new depths of boredom. Viewing figures were one million people a night down on the previous series, with more watching the opening night than the final. The votes cast were substantially down on previous years, the 4.3 million cast in the final week of *Big Brother* 4 being only half the figure of the previous series.

Nevertheless, it was still Channel Four's highest-rated show for the year, and they have contracted the show for another two series. There is talk of a *Champion Big Brother Special*, with the previous contestants taking part, throwing up the intriguing possibility of the likes of Nick Bateman, Jade Goody and Cameron Stout all playing happy families together. A ratings winner, and boasting hardcore fans (a record 10,000 people sent in home videos to audition for the fourth series), it seems that *Big Brother* will be with us for a while yet.

Federico is up for eviction and his mum Helen just can't wait for the whole thing to be over. Speaking at the family home in Glasgow she admitted: 'To be honest I hardly watch the show as I find it boring'.[1]

During the third series of *Big Brother* there was a lot of comment in the press that it had all rather degenerated since its heady start. It wouldn't be unfair to accuse the show of some cynical moves: supplying the contestants with gallons of drink and then filming the results, for starters. It's all very well showing us PJ and Jade after a ten-hour drinking session, but doesn't the show have some responsibility towards the contestants? It's easy television to ply the contestants with drink and then sit back and watch what they get up to. Even 'Nasty Nick' Bateman from the first series described the show as 'orchestrated' and 'manipulative'.

And, of course, all reality TV is edited. With dozens of cameras and constant filming, the editors have to show selected highlights. They can portray people in the light they want. When these don't tie in with participants' views of themselves there is bound to be controversy. Certainly a number of contestants from different series of the show are considering legal action after alleging that the selective editing left them damaged and prone to paranoia and depression over their spoilt career prospects and personal lives.

Criticism of the third series was overshadowed, though, by Jade Goody, who, despite not winning the £70,000 first prize, was the undoubted star of the show. Viewers saw her warts and all. They watched her in stand-up rows with a variety of housemates over issues as vital as fungal infections and what people might be saying about her. We saw her fumbling under the duvet with PJ after a ten-hour drinking session, courtesy of Channel Four, which thoughtfully provided us with night-sight cameras. Some of the voting public loved her; others hated her.

Then, much to everyone's surprise, *Big Brother* 4 was won by a Bible-reading virgin from the Orkneys. You would have been hard-pressed to script that, when the *Sun* was offering £50,000 to the first couple to have sex on the show. Yet there was something about Cameron and the way he lived his life that clearly attracted the voters. A series widely feared to plumb new depths of depravity was won by a Christian fish-trader. Reality TV turned out to be stranger than fiction.

What are we like?
Given the down-market goings on in the house, it might strike you as strange that this book talks about the series at all. What does *Big Brother* have to do with anything? Is it included here simply to provide something salacious? Well, I promise that isn't the case.

The reason we're talking about *Big Brother* is that I think the show gives us some pointers to human nature. Not only does watching the people in the house tell us something about human nature; so does the fact that so many of us watched it.

Jesus, in talking to the contestants and the viewers of *Big Brother*, would want to talk about this fundamental question, 'What are we like as human beings?' What does the show tell us about human nature?

This wider question is one that a lot of people have put their minds to. Many people throughout history have tried to work out what we are like:

> I have found little that is 'good' about human beings on the whole. In my experience most of them are trash. (Sigmund Freud)

> Two things are infinite: the universe and human stupidity; and I'm not sure about the universe. (Albert Einstein)

> Of mankind we may say in general they are fickle, hypocritical and greedy of gain. (Niccolo Machiavelli)

> If man had created man, he would be ashamed of his performance. (Mark Twain)

Quotes like these tell us something we already know: a lot of people are essentially very cynical about human nature. In fact, it's not that easy to find quotations in which people have positive things to say about humankind. There is this famous one from William Shakespeare, though:

> What a piece of work is a man! How noble in reason! how infinite in faculty! in form, in moving, how express and admirable! in action how like an angel! in apprehension how like a god!

It's certainly positive, but perhaps a tad idealistic? 'In action how like an angel!' I wonder if Shakespeare would have written such words in *Hamlet* if he'd watched *Big Brother*?

Jesus, of course, has far more of an idea about human nature than the jaded cynics or the blind optimism of Hamlet. He wouldn't need to watch the show to know what we are like. He'd be able to point us to parts of the Bible that he read, the Old Testament, to show us the fundamental flaw in us.

There's something wrong with human nature
The most famous example of bad behaviour from the show is still Nasty Nick, the villain of the first series. He became a figure of hate, someone who lied and cheated his way through the show. In the end he was confronted about his behaviour by Craig, a builder who wasn't expected to do very well in the show. This final showdown was the turning point for Craig in the house. Within a week he turned from a 20/1 outsider to the 5/4 favourite to win.

Nick claims that he was misrepresented and unfairly cast as the villain, and wrote a book giving his side of the story. Yet, as with Jade and the others, there has to be some truth in the way that they were portrayed. They obviously did the things that they were portrayed as doing.

In asking, 'What are we like?', I want to suggest that we are all a bit like Nasty Nick.

If his 'crimes' while in the house don't seem too great, perhaps it's because they weren't. Nick was the man who dared to commit the terrible crime of bringing a pencil into the house. It was a clear breach of the rules, but it was hardly a hanging offence. He was warned, both verbally and in writing, by Big Brother about his attempts to manipulate the voting. He told lie after lie to the other contestants, including a bizarre fiction in which he claimed that his wife had died in a car accident, presumably to get the sympathy vote.

Perhaps it seems a bit harsh to expel Nick for breaking the rules. After all, it was only a game show and it was only a pencil. But the rules were clear and he broke them. And all the other contestants agreed that he should go, too.

Aren't we all a bit like Nick? Certainly, by the time we had hit the third series, there were widespread attempts to break the rules imposed by *Big Brother*. Tim urged open rebellion, and Jade, Spencer and others were given formal warnings for breaking the rules. Even the eventual winner of series three, Kate, was fined six cans of lager for attempting to sneak drink to those on the wrong side of the divide created between rich and poor in the house.

The Bible confirms that we are all prone to breaking the rules. This is what the Bible means by that word 'sin'. 'Sin' isn't primarily about the things you read about in the front pages of the tabloids. It's the way we've made mistakes, sometimes by accident, sometimes on purpose. For example, can we say we've kept the Ten Commandments perfectly? These are the ten instructions God gave to his people after he'd rescued them from Egypt, in the Old Testament (Exodus 20:1–17). They aren't rules we're supposed to keep in order to be made right with God, but the standards of behaviour God expects from his people.

THE TEN COMMANDMENTS
 1 Don't have other gods.
 2 Don't make idols for yourself.
 3 Don't misuse God's name.
 4 Keep the Sabbath holy.
 5 Honour your parents.
 6 Don't murder.
 7 Don't commit adultery.
 8 Don't steal.
 9 Don't lie.
 10 Don't covet.

None of us can claim to have never broken the rules. None of us is perfect. In the language of the Bible, we're all sinners.

And, of course, we deny it. Most of us figure we've lived pretty good lives. We're not that bad, and we can usually point to someone who is a lot worse than we are. Our reactions to such an accusation are just like Nick's.

Confronted by his housemates about his behaviour, Nick

denied it. He lied to cover his tracks. When this didn't wash, he tried to justify his behaviour – after all, it was only a game show. Then, in an exclusive interview with *The Sun* (ironically, the tabloid that had been campaigning against him all summer), he was reported as having said, 'The word "cheat" is a nasty word and I don't believe I am one. I bent the rules – so what?'

> Tania was caught thieving cake, chocolate footballs and some sherbet from the Reward Room. When asked if she understood the rules, Tania looked puzzled and said sheepishly, 'I don't understand.' But the pretence couldn't be kept up for long and she broke into a cheeky grin. 'I am so lying!', she admitted.[2]
>
> *Big Brother*, series four

It's exactly this sort of behaviour that the Bible describes in pointing out the problem with us as human beings. What would Jesus say to the contestants of *Big Brother* and to each of us who watch it? I think he'd reveal that he knew exactly why it was that we all act in that way. Again, the Old Testament would be where he would show us this.

Right at the beginning of the Bible we read the account of Adam and Eve. In Genesis 2 – 3 we read that God created men and women in order to have a relationship with them. People seem to be the pinnacle of the creation, with responsibility to work the land and rule over the rest of creation. There's only one restriction to the way that Adam and Eve are to live: there's one tree whose fruit they should not eat.

No surprise, then, to find out what happens. First Eve, then Adam, eats the fruit. They break the rules. It's much more serious than breaking the rules of a game show; they've disobeyed God. And when they are confronted with the truth, they react in exactly the same way that Nasty Nick did and in exactly the same way that we tend to. They blame someone else.

So we're all a bit like Nick – we've broken the rules. And we tend to live in denial about it. We deny that we've done anything wrong, we try to justify it, or we decide (despite not being the injured party) that it doesn't matter. After all, we say, we're only human, or we were drunk, or people don't understand our situation. And we try to redefine what we've done. We haven't cheated; we've bent the rules. So that makes it all right, then!

We're not all bad
If you're thinking about whether the Christian message is true or not, you might have expected to hear that we're like Nick – that we are a bad bunch of people. But that's only part of the story and we know it. There's more to us than that. We're not all bad. If we were, *Big Brother* would have ended in bloodshed, and we'd have got a kick out of watching it. That didn't happen (though who knows what a future series will bring?).

However, there's another side to human nature, and I'm sure Jesus would present a balanced picture of how we are. You see, there are still aspects of our character that reflect the way God made us in the first place.

In watching the show we see that there are numerous examples of good acts in the house. Living in its pressure-cooker environment, there are times when people are just about hanging on or on the verge of walking out. In the game-show context, where the last person in the house is the winner, it might be considered surprising that the housemates support one another in the way they do. When arguments inevitably break out, others in the house often try to broker a reconciliation. When a housemate can't stand it for another day, others in the house try to talk them out of leaving.

As well as these small, everyday gestures of kindness, which all of us are capable of and practise, there are the less frequent, major good things that we are able to do. In the first series, Craig did a great thing when he gave away the £70,000 first prize to a girl who needed the money to go to the States to have an operation that she couldn't have in Britain. Having endured ten weeks in the pressured environment of the house, he simply handed over the cheque he was presented with as the winner. Few of us would have made such a gesture.

This is hardly rocket science, is it? We know that we're all capable of doing good things, and do actually do good things for other people. We help one another out, we support one another, we give to charity.

So when I talk about us all being sinners – people who have broken the rules – I also know that we're capable of great good too. Again, Genesis helps us to understand this. It tells us we are made in God's image. Part of what that must mean is that we're moral creatures, capable of great good.

We're a confusing contradiction. Even at our best, when we might want to do good things, we often fail. At the same time, when we might not want to do bad things, we sometimes still do them. That's how the apostle Paul described his own life in a letter to one of the churches: 'I don't understand myself at all, for I really want to do what is right, but I don't do it. Instead, I do the very thing I hate.'[3]

We're all capable of great things because we are created in God's image. But the problem is, that image gets distorted because we've broken the rules. God's image in us is marred by our rebellion.

We can't pretend that Nick is simply nasty and that Craig and Cameron are complete saints. It's not that clear-cut. Each of us is a contradiction. As the philosophers McCartney and Jackson put it, 'There's good and bad in everyone.'[4] Interestingly, the stylists who attended to Jade on a photoshoot for *Heat* magazine had her dressed as two different characters, 'angel Jade' and the 'red devil look', which the stylists said reflected Jade's personality in the house.

Now I know that very few of us have consciously rebelled, but in living life the way we figure we should, rather than the way our Creator says we should, we've rebelled. We've effectively said to God, 'I'll do life my own way, thank you very much.' In fact, that's such a common way of living that it might come as a complete shock to you even to consider that you should live life any other way. Each of us is as guilty of rebellion as the *Big Brother* contestants who band together to try to force the hand of the producers of the show.

Big Brother, and shows like it, fascinate us because they are first and foremost people shows. We get to see other people close up and can't get caught staring. We see how other people live their lives; we see the good and the bad in others. And if we're honest about it we can identify with the people we are watching. We see good and bad in the people we watch. We see a mirror that shows us what we are like.

Big Brother is television heroin: addictive, full of garbage, and distinguished by the fact that those who consume it are as degraded by the experience as those who peddle it.[5]

What would Jesus say about *Big Brother*? I think he'd point out our human nature. We're a bit like Nick; we've broken the rules. We're a bit like Craig; we're capable of enormous good. We're all just like Jade, a mixture of both good and bad. There's something not quite right with us.

But what about you and me?

Let's think beyond the contestants. What does it say about those who play the part of Big Brother? Interestingly, in Big Brother's Diary Room, the voice of the programme is sometimes referred to as 'the Voice of God'. Using this device, the makers of the programme were able to guide, control and communicate with the contestants. They used the Diary Room to rule on contentious issues. As with the outside world, some listened to 'the Voice of God' and did as they were advised. Others ignored the rules and didn't live in the way they were asked to. Are the producers of *Big Brother*, with their power to edit and present events as they wish, playing God?

Or are we, the viewing public, better cast in that role? After all, we have the power; the fate of the nominees lies in our hands. We dial one number and Nush gets the push. Dial a different one and it's 'Bye-bye, Jon.' Or do the media have the lion's share of power in all this? We could argue about who controls the show. Whatever we conclude, Jesus might well want to point to part of the most famous sermon anyone has ever preached:

> 'Do not judge, or you too will be judged. For in the same way as you judge others, you will be judged, and with the measure you use, it will be measured to you.
>
> 'Why do you look at the speck of sawdust in your brother's eye and pay no attention to the plank in your own eye? How can you say to your brother, "Let me take the speck out of your eye," when all the time there is a plank in your own eye? You hypocrite, first take the plank out of your own eye, and then you will see clearly to remove the speck from your brother's eye.'[6]

Big Brother might be a bit of fun, but we need to be careful because it encourages us to stand in judgment over others. And if we carry that into our daily life (and some of us don't need encouraging), we're in trouble. In life, says Jesus, if we spend our time being judgmental about people, we can guarantee that they will return the favour. Judge others and you'll be judged. So don't be so willing to point out the little faults of others when you probably have greater ones yourself. It's tempting to play God, but those of us who are keenest to draw attention to the faults of others should spend some time looking in the mirror first.

Incredibly, God sees and is able to judge, and yet doesn't rush to condemn, because he cares for us and loves us deeply. In that, God is very different from us, the media or the producers of *Big Brother*.

What's God like?
The producers who took it in turn to play the part of Big Brother had a list of set responses they could make. They seemed to be mostly, 'Big Brother will get back to you on that.' In the show Big

Brother wasn't allowed to intervene. (There were rare occasions when Big Brother entered the house, such as when the chip pan caught fire while everyone was in the garden and Security had to come and put it out for them.) The whole point was that Big Brother put the people in the house so that he could sit tight, watch them and see what happened.

Some people think God is just like that. He set up the world as some kind of experiment, and sat back, completely detached from us, to see what would happen.

That's the view of a couple of alleged psychologists who have written a light-hearted book called *You Are Worthless*. This is what they say: 'If there were a God, who was all powerful, all knowing and all seeing, he wouldn't give a rat's ass about you.'[7]

The Bible tells a very different story. It says you couldn't matter more. It makes a staggering central claim.

It's this: that God looked at what was going on all over his planet, and he didn't like what he saw. He saw all the law-breaking and the way the world is, and then showed us that Big Brother and God are very different. The God of the Bible is willing and able to intervene when he sees that we are threatened by something far more dangerous than a burning chip pan. More dangerous than a house fire? Yes! We are all in danger of ignoring the most important relationship we could ever enjoy, our relationship with our Maker.

The central message of the Christian faith is that God sent his only Son to get involved in his creation. The most famous sentences in the Bible summarize what it is all about:

> For God so loved the world that he gave his one and only Son, that whoever believes in him shall not perish but have eternal life. For God did not send his Son into the world to condemn the world, but to save the world through him.[8]

God sent his Son to intervene. Jesus didn't come to read us the riot act and knock heads together. He didn't come to jab an accusing finger in our faces and say, 'You've really messed up, haven't you? You're in for it now!'

Instead of coming to condemn us, Jesus came to save us.

It wasn't because of how lovely we are. He didn't come to save just the good ones, those who go to church and are nice to their families; those who are respectable. No. It says here that '*whoever* believes in him shall not perish but have eternal life' – anyone, whatever their background.

Why? Because 'God so loved the world . . .'

Jesus came to save us because God loves us. That's what God is like. It's in God's nature; he's like a loving father. The following chapters will spell this out in more detail as we try to get to grips with the enormity of this claim.

3

What would Jesus say 2:
Homer Simpson?

We need a nation closer to *The Waltons* than *The Simpsons*.
George Bush Sr

The world's favourite yellow family

Starting as a cartoon in the *Tracey Ullman Show*, *The Simpsons* soon outgrew their slot and became a smash-hit show in its own right. Fifteen years and more than 300 episodes later, America's first family is still going strong, and the commissioning of two new series in 2003 makes it the longest-running comedy in American history. In a UK poll of the favourite children's TV programmes of all time, conducted by Channel Four in 2001, *Mr Benn*, *Bagpuss* and the like were all beaten to the top spot by *The Simpsons*. I have to confess that I was a little surprised; not because of the quality of the show: I need no convincing of its brilliance. I just never thought of it as a children's show. I guess it's a mark of how far Matt Groening has taken the cartoon format. Cartoons always used to be for children; now, animation of this wit and quality is recognized as an art form for adults.

In the beginning there was quite a debate over the way faith was depicted on *The Simpsons*. We were warned of the dangers of the show and the likelihood that Bart Simpson would corrupt our nation's children. George Bush Sr commented in 1992 that 'we need a nation closer to *The Waltons* than *The Simpsons*'. This only led to Bart hitting back in a later episode with the quip that, just like *The Waltons*, his family was 'praying for an end to the Depression, too'. As critic Tom Carson comments, 'There was the President of The United States arguing with a cartoon. And losing.' [1] Ten years later the Simpsons were still courting controversy when a Catholic watchdog objected to a number of adverse references to its religion in *The Simpsons*, unusually causing the show to re-edit an episode.

These days, though, this is very much an exception. The show is generally feted by religious academics for the positive way that it portrays faith. The series' executive producer, Mike Scully, says that 'the show tries to reflect through its characters the fact that faith plays a substantial part in many families' lives, although it is seldom portrayed on television'. [2] Now, Rowan Williams, Archbishop of Canterbury, endorses Mark Pinsky's book *The Gospel According to The Simpsons* – something that would have been unthinkable when Bush made his comment.

What happened? What caused this amazing turnabout? How did Homer and his house turn from being public religious enemy number one to becoming the acceptable face of faith on national television? Well, I don't know that the *series* changed, but we started watching it; perhaps it's as simple as that.

When we did, we found that Scully's words were true: *The Simpsons*, unlike most other TV shows, reflects the fact that issues of faith play a strong part in the lives of many people. It also portrays the fact that, even in little old Springfield, there are many different expressions of faith. There's Apu, the Hindu storekeeper, and Krusty, the Jewish clown. There's the jaundiced Rev. Lovejoy, who never displays the attributes you'd expect given his calling and his surname. There is, of course, Ned Flanders, the almost relentlessly chirpy born-again neighbour of the Simpsons. And, of course, the Simpsons themselves. They pray, they go to church and they debate ethical issues all the time as, like all families, they try to work out how they should live.

We also found a funny, clever show that isn't afraid to laugh at the failings of organized religion but is far from vindictive in its humour. Take the Rev. Lovejoy, for example. He is lampooned for his woolly beliefs and that fact that he doesn't own a Bible but borrows his copy from the public library. He despairs of the zealousness of Ned Flanders and trains his dog to do its business on Ned's lawn. Hardly a shining advertisement for the ministry! Rev. Lovejoy's life doesn't match up, and as such he's a fair target for the satirists; even then, he is hardly pilloried the way he might be; the humour is far from cruel.

Ned is mocked for his unfailing and irritating cheerfulness. Homer is rude beyond belief to him, and yet Ned is, with very few exceptions, always resoundingly loving in the face of the provocation from his neighbour. When the show pokes fun at Ned, it's gentle and often deserved. He's left as the sole exception in the show, in that 'He is incapable of cynicism or contempt, unlike just about everybody else in town'.[3] Even in his frustration with his neighbour, Homer's insults don't get much ruder (or ignorant) than 'He's holier than Jesus'.

This man has turned every cheek on his body. If everyone here were like Ned Flanders, there'd be no need for heaven: we'd already be there.

Homer J. Simpson, theologian

One of the great strengths of *The Simpsons* is its cartoon format. Cartoons give a licence to do all sorts of things that a regular show couldn't do without distracting us from how ludicrous the concept might be. So when Bono or Rupert Murdoch or Michael Jackson turns up in Springfield, well, why not? As a result, when Homer meets and talks with God, no-one bats an eyelid. It's a cartoon, surreal and escapist; why shouldn't such a thing happen? *The*

Simpsons can address the big issues in life. Devices can be brought into play to transport the characters into the past or future; they can meet God or the devil and visit heaven or hell. *The Simpsons* takes full advantage of the format and can ask some big questions about life through the cartoon.

What's that faith again?

So what would Jesus have to say to Homer Simpson? He's the Duff-drinking, doughnut-eating employee of a nuclear power plant who tries to do the best by his family, often letting down his wife and kids in the process. Jesus might well start by making some introductions, because Homer has a basic problem with his faith. He is pretty hazy about what or who it is that he believes in. And in that he's typical of many of us. It might well reflect the preaching at Springfield Community Church that, although the family seem to be a Protestant Christian family, attending church and praying on a regular basis, they don't seem to have much idea about who Jesus is. Homer's theology isn't exactly well developed. At one point, in defending his actions in abandoning the church, Homer responds, 'Kids, let me tell you about another so-called wicked guy. He had long hair and some wild ideas. He didn't always do what other people thought was right. And that man's name was ... I forget.' It gets even worse when, in great danger, Homer cries out to Jesus, but gets his name wrong!

'Perfect teeth. Nice smell. A class act, all the way.'
Homer J. Simpson on God

There are other little indicators too, such as when Homer asks his wife, 'What's the name of that religion with all the well-meaning rules that don't work in real-life?' As well as revealing that he's so dense that he can't remember the name of the faith he is supposed to be following, this shows us that Homer considers himself something of a pragmatist when it comes to matters of faith. When he's approached by a stranger in an airport and urged to 'do unto others as you would have them do unto you', Homer dismisses the man with a sarcastic, 'That'll work.'

It's exaggerated, of course, but isn't it essentially how many people feel about their faith? While few people who would consider themselves Christians would struggle to name their religion, there's a lot of Homer in our feelings about our faith. Faced with a form to fill in, we might write 'C of E' or 'Baptist', but just don't ask us to explain what that means. In the same way, we might admire many of the teachings of the faith, but, like Homer, we doubt whether it actually works. It sounds like a fine theory, but we wouldn't want to stake our lives on it.

Of course, we're glad that it's there for when we need it. Like the characters in the show when they are in any kind of trouble, we'll pray, though we may not be sure of how to pray or who to pray to.

'Hey, I'm not a bad guy!'

When Jesus has made some basic introductions, he might go on to commend Homer for some of the things that he does. You might expect Homer to be condemned, but there is much about him that deserves praise.

He's a guy who, in the main, tries to do the right thing. When he's tempted to have an affair with a country singer, he resolves, in the face of great temptation, to stay true to Marge. When Lisa wants a pony, Homer gets a second job in order to try to accommodate her wish. Even when he has gone the wrong way, he draws back from complete disaster, usually due to the good influence of Marge. It's under her guidance that he gives up his illegal cable TV hook-up. He even brings himself to forgive her for spoiling his chances of a million-dollar payout when Bart sustains minor injuries in an accident.

Of course, part of the reason why Jesus might need to make some basic introductions is that the church has let him down pretty badly. Homer, like so many of us, has a problem with church. As he is quick to point out to God in one episode, 'I'm not a bad guy! I work hard and I love my kids. So why should I spend half my Sunday hearing about how I'm going to hell? ... I figure I should try to live right and worship you in my own way.' Typically, Homer decides that the way to do that is to start his own religion, one that doesn't saddle him with the inconvenience of going to church.

More tea, Vicar?
To be fair, given the kind of church that Homer goes to, you might not blame him for being less than ecstatic about being there on a Sunday. Rev. Lovejoy is hardly the most charismatic church leader in history. Let's be frank here: he seems jaded and uninspired. From what we hear of his Easter Sunday sermon, it's more about chocolate bunnies than the resurrection of Jesus. In another service, Lovejoy is seemingly in full flow, only to miss the point completely: 'I remember another gentle visitor from the heavens. He came in peace and then died, only to come back to life. And his name was E.T.' Neither would you rush to him for counselling. Marge takes on most of the pastoral work when Rev. Lovejoy doesn't want to do it any more, and he reflects that she 'taught me that there's more to being a minister than not caring about people'. Ouch! As a church minister myself, that's a bit close to the mark.

Given the general malaise that surrounds Springfield Community Church, why should anyone want to get involved? Perhaps that's a feeling that you can all too readily identify with. When church looks like this, or like the congregation in that episode where Mr Bean goes to church, or in pretty much any TV depiction, why bother taking part in something so irrelevant? Why should Homer keep going along every week when he could stay at home and enjoy himself, as he does in the classic episode, 'Homer the Heretic'?

Marge: 'Homer, the Lord only asks for an hour a week.'
Homer: 'In that case he should have made the week an hour longer. Lousy God!'

Eating for eternity

What would Jesus have to say to Homer Simpson? Perhaps he'd talk to him about heaven. I suspect that Homer would be completely sceptical about such a place at first, but Jesus would know just how to get his attention. From the way Jesus describes it, Homer would like heaven. It's described as a wedding banquet,[4] and with all the food and drink that this would involve you can be sure that Homer would be a fan.

Similarly, heaven is described as a party. Some of the parables that Jesus told make it clear that heaven is going to be a great celebration. He told stories about a shepherd who rejoices over finding his lost sheep, and about a woman who throws a party when she finds the ten per cent of her wealth that she had thought she had lost.

'Suppose one of you has a hundred sheep and loses one of them. Does he not leave the ninety-nine in the open country and go after the lost sheep until he finds it? And when he finds it, he joyfully puts it on his shoulders and goes home. Then he calls his friends and neighbours together and says, "Rejoice with me; I have found my lost sheep." I tell you that in the same way there will be more rejoicing in heaven over one sinner who repents than over ninety-nine righteous persons who do not need to repent.

'Or suppose a woman has ten silver coins and loses one. Does she not light a lamp, sweep the house and search carefully until she finds it? And when she finds it, she calls her friends and neighbours together and says, "Rejoice with me; I have found my lost coin." In the same way, I tell you, there is rejoicing in the presence of the angels of God over one sinner who repents.'[5]

Knowing that heaven is a party with the chance to celebrate and enjoy good and (perhaps more importantly for Homer) plentiful food and drink would be a great thrill to Homer. And to think that this is the deal for all eternity! Probably such abundance and sheer joy would be the last thing that Homer would expect from anything associated with the church. Sadly, most people would probably have the same view.

How does Homer get to heaven?

Homer is basically a good guy who tries to do the right thing – sometimes. He often has good intentions, but is frighteningly weak as soon as any temptation concerning food is involved. Which is why he'd like the sound of heaven; he'd almost be tempted to be virtuous! But how does he get there? Of all the questions addressed by the show, perhaps one of the key ones is, 'What do I have to do to get to heaven?' How does Homer get to the party?

You don't expect the show to provide the answers to that kind of question, of course. Lest we forget, we are dealing with a cartoon here, albeit a funny, serious and profound one. When the show flirts with such weighty questions it obviously does so for their comic potential. Thus Bart and Homer watch a TV movie in which God says to Noah, 'Remember, the key to salvation is ...', only for a news bulletin to cut in that very moment. Similarly, when Bart meets the devil and asks how he can avoid going to hell, he's told that he wouldn't want to know, and that Bart should 'lie, cheat, steal and listen to heavy metal music' instead.

All the same, this is an informative exchange, because it contains the popular idea that so many in Springfield and so many of us believe: namely, that the way to get to heaven is to keep the rules and avoid sin. This is highlighted a number of times and even seems to be the teaching of the church in Springfield. Perhaps it's something that you've picked up, too.

When Martin, the particularly keen child in Sunday School who is scared half witless by a description of life in hell, asks how to 'steer clear of the abode of the damned', he is told to 'do good works and avoid sin'. A number of times Ms Albright, the Sunday School teacher, tells her young charges that if people are good they go to heaven. Although it runs completely counter to the official teaching of any Protestant church (which is what Springfield

Community Church appears to be), this is nevertheless what is taught there.

It's also the message that most people in nominally Christian countries have picked up. The way they see it, it's all very straightforward. The good guys go to heaven, while the baddies go to ... well, they go somewhere else, because, I mean, who actually believes in hell any more, except as a place for evil dictators, perverts and murderers?

The reasoning follows that part of being a good guy is going to church. This is neatly illustrated in the episode of *The Simpsons* where Homer becomes an accidental missionary. No, really! Unsure as he is about the nature of his God, he's uncertain what to do in this role. He decides to lead the people in constructing a church building. Upon admiring the completed building, he reflects, 'I may not know much about God, but I have to say we built a pretty nice cage for him.'

There is, of course, a great deal more to worshipping God than putting up a building. An argument then develops between the islanders about how often they must attend services in order to avoid going to hell. In response to the proposal, 'Every Sunday for the rest of our lives', an islander laughs and asks for a serious answer.

It's a desperately sad picture. The image here is of a God who will judge his people by weighing the good deeds against the dodgy ones and then, hopefully, find in our favour. Keeping God happy involves the dull rigmarole of being in church every Sunday. If you can stay awake for the whole hour, so much the better.

It may be a sad picture, but it's the one that many people have of God today: if you can be good and go to church, you'll be OK for the afterlife – although, if that consists of sitting around on a cloud with a harp for all eternity, we can't get too excited about it.

 Everybody's a sinner except this guy.
Homer J. Simpson, Bible reader

What would Jesus have to say to the Simpsons about the message of Christianity? I think that he'd want to talk to them about how they can't get to heaven in the way they think. There's more to being a Christian than trying your best and going to church.

Most of us try our best, whether we'd consider ourselves religious or not. Some of us are better at being good than others. We might be kind to others, or give money to charity on a regular basis. We might be able to go for months without swearing, and have no criminal record. We might have helped those in need or managed to run a marathon for charity.

There's nothing wrong with any of these actions; they are good things to do. Homer does his best to do great deeds for his children, as we do for ours. But the Bible teaches us that all these things, good as they are in our own eyes, aren't as great we like to think they are. You see, it's in our nature to underestimate the seriousness of our sin. We might think we're OK, and that if God takes the top fifty per cent we have a good chance of heaven. When we think like that, we have no idea of the deadly seriousness of sin so far as God is concerned. God sees our situation very differently. The Old Testament prophet Isaiah gives us an insight into this:

> We are all infected and impure with sin. When we proudly display our righteous deeds, we find they are but filthy rags. Like autumn leaves, we wither and fall. And our sins, like the wind, sweep us away.[6]

These are radical thoughts. The Bible says that we are all unclean in God's eyes. Our sins are all those thoughts, acts and words that offend God. Each one of us sins; you, me, anyone you care to name. There are no exceptions. Notice that even our righteous acts, or good deeds, are like filthy rags before God. All our good deeds, which we think are so important, are just dirty laundry in God's eyes.

All those little transgressions that we thought were so unimportant turn out to matter a great deal. So the first message of Christianity is that we are in desperate trouble, because none of us measures up in God's sight. So far, so bad.

Is it hopeless for Homer, then?

If our best endeavours are no use whatsoever and just compound the problem, what can we do? Not a lot. That's the whole point. It took something out of the ordinary to bring about a solution to this problem. It needed someone capable of true greatness, someone who could live a spotless life and then take on all the dross of everyone else in order to release them from the bondage of sin and its effects.

Central to the Christian faith is the fact that Jesus Christ came and did just that. In his life and death, Jesus paved the way for our rescue. You see the difference? While most religion, in Springfield or elsewhere, is a matter of what we do, Christianity is about what Jesus has done.

He did it for people like Homer Simpson – people who drink too much Duff beer and live lives that don't come up to scratch. He did it for people who try their best to bring up their kids and stay faithful to their loved ones and have, at best, a patchy record in doing the right thing.

'I want to share something with you – the three little sentences that will get you through life. Number one: "Cover for me." Number two: "Oh, good idea, boss." Number three: "It was like that when I got here."'
Homer J. Simpson, responsible parent

So, is there any hope for Homer? Actually, I think Homer has a lot of hope. He may not know much about his God. He may not care much for being in church on a Sunday morning. He may let his family and friends down regularly. But there is definitely hope for him. Why? Precisely because he knows he's a mess.

One of Jesus' most devastating stories shows there's hope for Homer and for those of us like him. Faced with a bunch of smug, self-satisfied religious leaders

> ... who were confident of their own righteousness and looked down on everybody else, Jesus told this parable: 'Two men went up to the temple to pray, one a Pharisee and the other a tax collector. The Pharisee stood up and prayed about himself: "God, I thank you that I am not like other men – robbers, evildoers, adulterers – or even like this tax collector. I fast twice a week and give a tenth of all I get."
>
> 'But the tax collector stood at a distance. He would not even look up to heaven, but beat his breast and said, "God, have mercy on me, a sinner."' [7]

This gives us two very different styles of prayer. You might recognize both attitudes. I wonder which one you can most readily identify with? The Pharisee was a respected and respectable holy man. Notice the words Jesus uses here: they explain what was wrong with the prayer of the religious leader. He 'prayed about himself'. He came before God very boldly and commended himself to his Maker. You get the impression that he thought God should be pleased to have him on his side. His religious CV compared his character with those around him and (surprise, surprise) he came out of it all rather well. He wasn't like other men – certainly not like this tax collector – and he fasted and gave a tenth of all that he had to God and his work. Wasn't he great?

The tax collector was a pretty miserable specimen compared with the Pharisee. He couldn't look up to heaven and sing his own praises in the way that this religious giant could. No, he didn't dare come too close to pray. Without even looking up into heaven he very simply asked, 'God, have mercy on me, a sinner.' Here was a man who was well aware of his own failings. He knew that his best efforts were still like dirty laundry in the eyes of the all-powerful and holy God. He knew he was a sinner, and that his life didn't measure up in the way it needed to.

I can see Homer in this parable. At his most stupid and deluded he thinks he's the greatest, but it never takes much to bring him down to earth with a bump, and then he sees himself for what he really is. At these times Marge is often there to offer him the unconditional love that is so vital in getting him through life. It's not hard to see Homer in this parable of Jesus; he's the guy at the back of the church, well aware of his faults and asking for mercy.

Jesus concludes the story in a way that must have shocked those who listened to him. 'I tell you, this sinner, not the Pharisee, returned home justified before God. For the proud will be humbled, but the humble will be honored.'[8]

This is why I believe there is hope for Homer. He knows what he's like. For all his faults, a lack of self-awareness isn't one of them. Jesus says to Homer here (and of course to each of us) that we need to come to God with a certain attitude: not like the Pharisee, thinking how great we are, but like the tax collector, realizing our limitations and asking for mercy. There's hope for Homer. There's hope for us all.

4

What would Jesus say 2:
Anne Robinson?

> Of course I drink in the bloody morning. Presuming I know that
> it is the morning.[1]
>
> *Anne Robinson, March 1973*

It's only a few paces, but the walk of shame that each of the failed
contestants in *Weakest Link* has to take must seem more like a
mile. It is the final humiliation in a show that specializes in
humiliating its contestants. There must almost be a sense of relief
for the departing loser. The payoff that rings in their ears – 'You
are the weakest link. Goodbye!' – at least has the merit of being
the final insult that they will have to endure from the person who
has been dubbed the rudest woman on British television.

Anne Robinson has a fantastic riches-to-rags-to-riches story to
tell, and she does so with great aplomb in her autobiography,
Memoirs of an Unfit Mother. After working as a journalist, making
her mark on the *Daily Mirror*, she moved into television and shone
as a TV presenter. It is, of course, *Weakest Link* that has stamped
her upon the nation's consciousness as contestants line up for the
chance to be humiliated in the hope of winning a couple of grand.

When NBC were looking to import the show to the United States they were shrewd enough to recognize that Anne Robinson *is* the show, and took an unheard-of risk by inviting her, though unknown in the States, to present the show for them. There, critics dubbed her 'the Queen of Mean' and 'the Host from Hell', and Mike Tyson (of all people!) told her, 'You're one mean woman.' She was also a tremendous ratings success, taking her shows in Britain and the US ever upwards.

> I never worked on my profile – you get what you see, exactly the same person you'd get if you came to dinner. I hope. I think I'm like marzipan, you either really like what I have to offer, or you hate it.

On the face of it, life has always been good for Anne. She was born into a background of great privilege. Her mother was a market trader in Liverpool, dealing in poultry. It may not sound that fancy, but the family supplied the hotels, ships, railways and restaurants across the area. The business was such a success that Anne recalls that she lived in ignorance about the hardships others were going through during the war. The family was enjoying 'juicy steaks, eggs galore, even bananas, during all the time the Germans had been razing Liverpool to the ground'.[2] Added to this were the annual holidays in the South of France, smuggling their money abroad so as to stay in the best hotel in Cannes for as long as six weeks at a time. Even today this is something most of us can only dream about, let alone in the 1940s and '50s, when foreign travel was relatively rare.

So, with such a great start in life and a career as one of the most famous quiz-show hosts ever, life has been a bed of roses for Anne, hasn't it? Well, it has, but only if you take into account all the thorns in the rosebed. Although you might never suspect it from her sneering performances as the Queen of Mean, there have been episodes in her life when Anne has been, most definitely, the weakest link.

Anne as the weakest link

Anne knows this. Her autobiography is very honest about those times. She's well aware of how she's made a mess of things on occasions. The headline-grabbing story was about the battles that she had as an alcoholic. Having grown up with an alcoholic mother, Anne reveals in graphic detail how, a generation later, she had the same battle with drink. It was a battle that wiped out large tracts of the 1970s for her. Reading her account, there is no doubt that her drinking exacted a terrible price:

> The fun stage of my drinking was short-lived compared to the ugly
> years. When it reached its worst it meant ending up with my knickers
> round my neck in a bed I did not recognize, surrounded by vomit and
> having not the faintest idea where I was.[3]

How does it feel to wake up in such a state? Anne talks about being disgusted with herself and deciding, with the logic of the alcoholic, that another drink was what was needed to quieten the demons. Once the off-licence was open at 8am, Anne would be there to buy vodka, so desperate to keep up appearances that she 'stood at home for the minutes leading up to eight o'clock, holding on to a chair in case she fell down, and practised handing over the money'.[4]

You can't read an account like that without having enormous sympathy for Anne. Given the nature of her autobiography, she doesn't paper over her faults when she's sober either. She draws attention to her stupidity and selfishness, declares that her 'impatience – still with me today – is neither wise nor admirable',[5] and acknowledges when writing of her relationship with her first husband that 'Our faults were massive. In times of fear and distress, decent human beings do bad things to each other.'[6]

What would Jesus have to say to Anne Robinson? As well as applauding her honesty, I think that he would affirm something of her experience from the Bible. People who are generally decent human beings (at least by the standards that we tend to use to judge decency) do terrible things to other people and indeed to themselves.

Jesus might well point us to Paul's observation, in his letter to the Roman church, that essentially all human beings are the same:

> We are made right in God's sight when we trust in Jesus Christ to take away our sins. And we all can be saved in this same way, no matter who we are or what we have done. For all have sinned; all fall short of God's glorious standard. Yet now God in his gracious kindness declares us not guilty. He has done this through Christ Jesus, who has freed us by taking away our sins.[7]

This word that the Bible uses for 'sin' is not one that we like to own. We know what sin is (we've read about it in the *News of the World*), but it doesn't really apply to us if we are decent and respectable citizens, does it? Well, according to the Bible, yes, it does. Sin is when we make a mess of something and fall short of God's perfect standards. It's not just that we sin in the bad things that we do, or in the good things that we leave undone. It's not just the awful things that we say to one another. It's not just our thoughts we're glad others don't even know about. It's all those things and more. It's the whole way that our lives tend to revolve around us and what we want, rather than having God at the centre. All this sin means there are times when we are the weakest link, and when we are guilty of falling short of our own standards, let alone God's – which, given his holiness, must be much higher than ours. We are *all* guilty of this. No exceptions.

By her own public admission – and that marks her out as a rare person – there have been times when Anne Robinson has been the weakest link. Don't think I'm getting at Anne. For a start, I'm nowhere near brave enough to pick on her! But throughout her account she is honest enough to highlight truths about herself and her life that don't always reflect well on her.

About two months later he turned up in London to confess that he was married. I went on yet another bender and ended up being collected by ambulance from a women's lavatory on the newsroom floor of the *Sunday Times*.[8]

We are all weak links

If Anne Robinson decided to write the story of your life she'd be able to uncover the same about you, and about me. The details would be different, but the essential facts would be the same: namely, that there are things in all of our lives that we aren't proud of, and are actually rather ashamed of. I'm very grateful that my flaws aren't public property. I don't need reminding that sin in the way that I live my life makes me the weakest link. Do you?

In case we need any more convincing, listen to how Jesus catalogues some of the ways we make a mess of things:

> 'For from within, out of a person's heart, come evil thoughts, sexual immorality, theft, murder, adultery, greed, wickedness, deceit, eagerness for lustful pleasure, envy, slander, pride, and foolishness. All these vile things come from within; they are what defile you and make you unacceptable to God.'[9]

It's quite some list, isn't it? If you're anything like me, you'll be tempted to skip over it quickly. Don't. Consider it carefully. Are you guilty of murder? Maybe, maybe not. Jesus warns that if you're even angry with your brother, you'd better be ready for judgment.[10] Are you guilty of adultery? Jesus tells us that anyone who looks lustfully at a woman has already committed adultery with her in his heart[11] – and I see no reason why it shouldn't apply to women looking lustfully at men too. There are some sins on that list that we don't even think are all that serious. Look at greed, envy, arrogance: they may not be very pleasant, but they aren't the end of the world, are they? After all, none of us is perfect.

Yet Jesus clearly sees these wrongs as being of the utmost importance; otherwise, we'd have to conclude that he's simply warning us for fun. These things that make us 'unclean' are what the Bible refers to elsewhere as sin. They are the actions and (as we see here) *thoughts* that separate us from God and make us unclean. We may not take them seriously; Jesus clearly does.

Having established that sin makes every single one of us weak links, what happens to us? As we know, the contestants in the quiz show are shown no mercy. Faced with their failure, they are insulted by their host for a final time and then go to give their parting interview, in which they invariably blame their opponents for ganging up on them or claim that it was unfair because they had harder questions than anyone else. Tells us something about human nature, doesn't it?

Is this how God reacts to our being the weakest link? Like the failed quiz contestants, we can't put things right for ourselves. Does Jesus come to identify our failings and then dismiss us into the outer darkness? He comes with far more authority than any quiz-show host could ever hope to muster, but the good news is that he is very different.

What to do with weak links?
Summing up what Jesus is all about, John, one of the disciples who knew him best, tells us:

> 'For God so loved the world that he gave his only Son, so that whoever believes in him will not perish but have eternal life. For God did not send his Son into the world to condemn it, but to save it.' [12]

Well aware that the world is populated by weak links, God faced a choice about what to do. Should he go the same way as Anne on her show? There the researchers do their job and find out all about the competitors. The victims are taunted before the nation, their weaknesses mercilessly drawn to our attention by Ms Robinson. Should God come along and escort us from the set? No.

John's verdict was that the opposite was true. Jesus knows each of us deeply, and yet, rather than use that information to dismiss us, he does the opposite and moves towards us. Instead of coming along to condemn us for the ways we have all fouled up, God sent his only Son to step in and do something to put it all right. He could have come and sorted us out once and for all, sneered at us and sent us packing. But God is revealed to be very different here. He sent his Son to rescue the weak links. As we saw when we looked at what Jesus would say to Homer Simpson, that means every last one of us.

One thing is for sure. Jesus doesn't sneer at our attempts to live a good life and dismiss us as the weakest link. Unlike Anne, his catchphrase would more likely be, 'You are the weakest link. Hello.' Why not take the chance to spend some time looking at what he said and did, and the claims he makes, and decide for yourself?

Sounds too good to be true, though, doesn't it? That was certainly my reaction when I first heard about this offer of Jesus' rescue. I'm sure the seasoned hack in Anne would cause her to want to look into this a lot further before accepting such lavish claims.

Needing a drink

The way that Jesus dealt with the people he met shows us that he isn't the sort to dismiss those who didn't measure up. Here's a classic illustration of that. One day, while his friends were shopping for food, Jesus stayed in a town called Sychar and rested there at the well because he was tired. When a Samaritan woman came along, Jesus struck up a conversation with her.

> Jesus, tired from the long walk, sat wearily beside the well about noontime. Soon a Samaritan woman came to draw water, and Jesus said to her, 'Please give me a drink.' [13]

Nothing unusual about that, you might think. You'd be wrong. The culture that Jesus lived in was very different from our own.

What Jesus did here broke all the conventions of the day. Certainly it came as a surprise to the woman!

> The woman was surprised, for Jews refuse to have anything to do with Samaritans. She said to Jesus, 'You are a Jew, and I am a Samaritan woman. Why are you asking me for a drink?' [14]

To understand how different Jesus is from many religious leaders today, consider how different he was from those he lived among.

There were some devout folk who wouldn't even go through Samaria when travelling from Judea to Galilee. Instead, they would go right out of their way in order not to have to pass through the land of the 'unclean' Samaritans. Jesus showed a very different attitude. He walked through Samaria.

Rabbis didn't usually talk to women. Some of them gave instruction such as 'It is forbidden to give a woman any greeting', and 'One should not talk to a woman on the street, not even with his own wife, and certainly not with someone else's wife, because of the gossip of men'. Maybe no-one told Jesus. More likely, he knew all about these attitudes and struck up a conversation with the woman anyway.

Women were often illiterate because they weren't given an education. A rabbi called Eliezer taught that 'If a man gives his daughter a knowledge of the law it is as though he taught her lechery'. It's a strange attitude. The good teaching about God and his law should not be taught to a woman? In contrast, Jesus has a deep spiritual conversation with the woman at the well.

Jesus had a different attitude from that of other religious teachers. The disciples found him talking to a Samaritan woman and were surprised, though they knew enough not to question him about it. He asked the woman for a drink of water. Again, this is surprising. If she drew the water for him it would technically have been ceremonially unclean. Jews wouldn't even use the same plates as Samaritans. It didn't seem to bother Jesus.

There are clues in the report of the meeting Jesus had with the Samaritan woman that suggest she was a social outcast. Yet Jesus clearly had time for her, and then made further time for her friends, staying a couple more days.[15] Jesus showed this woman nothing but courtesy. Clearly, there is something about the way Jesus deals with us that is very unlike the way other people deal with us.

Jesus' attitude was not what we might expect. This woman had been married to five men and was living with a sixth. We know this was the case because Jesus, with his incredible insight into her life, told her this was so. Doesn't Jesus have something to say to people living like that? Of course he does, but he doesn't seem to feel the need to wade in and destroy her by condemning her failings. He simply sits down and starts a conversation with her. He shows her a level of respect and compassion that she'd have found very unusual in the men she'd known.

We must celebrate our strengths, work around our weaknesses. We must throw in our lot together. Trust was important. Or as my friend Jill Foot, now no longer around to nod her approval, might have said, 'Make his happiness more important than your own'. Nothing remarkable about that, you might think. It is what *for better or for worse* is all about. It is how the most enduring and successful partnerships work, be it in marriage, in business, in friendship, in families. But it had taken me a lifetime to understand it.[16]

Anne Robinson on marriage

Oh, for an unconditional love!

This Samaritan outcast, a prime candidate for being the weakest link, wasn't treated to a put-down and a lonely walk of shame. She was listened to by the one man who loved her differently from the way any man had ever loved her before. It's a love that accepts another person regardless of what they might have done and how they might be living. It's a love that's easier to write and dream about than to put into practice. But Jesus managed it. Anne is realistic about how rare that kind of love is, and declares it's not even something you can expect to find in marriage:

> Every young woman needs a cushion that says: 'No one is coming along to rescue you'. No one gives you unconditional love except your mother and then only sometimes. The sassy career girl is free to plan her romantic white wedding with all the enthusiasm of an immature adolescent but woe betide her if she thinks her husband is going to fill every gap in her life. When he turns out to be human she may be disappointed. She should not be surprised.[17]

That's the whole thing about unconditional love – it's so hard to love like that. You might well think marriage is the one place where you could expect to find unconditional love, and ideally you do. But, as Anne astutely notes, no husband or wife is going to fill every gap in your life. She even identifies why it doesn't always work the way it should. The problem is yours and mine. We're human. And human beings don't always love unconditionally.

Each of us knows what it feels like to be let down by another person. Each of us knows what it feels like to let down someone else. There are times in our lives when we are the weakest link, and our relationships have suffered the consequences of such (bad) behaviour. Broken promises, broken hearts and broken relationships testify to this. In other cases the relationship continues but is never the same as it was before. Those careless words, that selfish action, ended up costing more than we ever thought. Thankfully, some manage to piece things back together. Please don't think that I'm referring only to romantic relationships. I'm thinking here of relationships in the widest sense. We mess them up with alarming frequency, because we are all weak links.

Only Jesus, who (incredibly) was both fully God in the flesh and yet also fully human, has perfectly and consistently managed this business of loving unconditionally. He, and he alone, is able and willing to love like that. He demonstrated it by the way he spoke with the woman at the well, to give just one example from among all the people he spent time with. He showed it ultimately by the nature of his death, as Paul wrote to his young co-worker Timothy:

> This is a true saying, and everyone should believe it: Christ Jesus came into the world to save sinners – and I was the worst of them all. But that is why God had mercy on me, so that Christ Jesus could use me as a prime example of his great patience with even the worst sinners. Then others will realize that they, too, can believe in him and receive eternal life.[18]

You might think that Jesus' death on a cross was a tragic end to the life of a good man. As with so many heroes, he died young, and it seems like a waste even though he lives on in a way that shows that his influence on the planet is greater than anyone else has ever had. Yet Jesus wasn't simply put to death against God's will. Astonishingly, it was all part of God's plan.

While the crucifixion might have looked like a victory for first-century politicians, it was in fact nothing of the sort. It was the ultimate expression of unconditional love, which sees God the Father holding back nothing, not even his one and only Son. That same unconditional love sees Jesus, God the Son, going to his death on a cross. Look at how God shows that unconditional love for you, for me, and for all of us weak links.

What does it mean that Christ died for us? What on earth does his death have to do with us? Simply put, it was God's way of rescuing us from an eternity spent disconnected from him. You see, there is a crucial point on which Anne Robinson is wrong. There *is* someone who shows unconditional love to us. He doesn't just teach what it looks like, or demonstrate it in the abstract, but directs it to each of us individually. Equally, there is someone who comes to rescue us. It was the whole reason why Jesus stepped into history. He offers to rescue us from a life spent without a right relationship with him and an eternity spent out of his presence. It's a rescue from a meaningless life spent disconnected from the very reason for our existence in this world. We were created to live with a relationship with God at the centre of our lives. It's the way that really works. The rescue offered to us is a rescue from the consequences of our choosing to do things our own way.

As with any rescue, it can be accepted or rejected. If you've been trapped or physically stuck in some way and needed to be rescued, you know that when your rescuer arrives you have a choice. Most of us don't have to think twice about it; we gladly accept the offer of help and are only too pleased to be rescued. A few might reject the offer out of hand. Others might feel they are not in any great danger and they have no need of rescue.

What you decide to do with this offer of rescue is entirely up to you. It's a decision only you can make. Having discovered that your actions have made you the weakest link, what will you choose to do about it?

What would Jesus say 2: Eminem?

A grown-up Bart Simpson without the benefit of Bart's loving, supportive family.[1]

Hero or villain?

The newspaper headlines are clear as to who the problem is, whether they can prove much of a link or not. 'Rapper's lyrics linked to fan's suicide'; 'Eminem's lyrics are blamed for sex attack'; 'Obsessive Eminem fan beat girlfriend with bicycle chain'.

Yet he's also feted by the white liberal establishment, who have described him as 'a kind of court jester of hip-hop', describing his work as 'a critical portrait of a murderous psyche; no more an endorsement of the misogyny that it presented than Browning's *My Last Duchess* is an endorsement of domestic violence'.[2] (Phew!) One critic even went so far as to say that 'the RSC could learn a thing or two at the moment from the clarity of his diction'.[3]

He has a tattoo expressing the wish that his former wife might rot in pieces. His lyrics with their expressed hatred of gays have upset homosexual pressure groups and seen him banned by universities. Peter Tatchell, famous for being, among other things, a gay-rights campaigner, compared him to Hitler. And yet, at the Grammys, Eminem sang a duet with the Queen Mum of rock, Sir Elton John, who embraced him on stage.

The critics applaud his 'extremely funny, angry readings of America's celebrity culture'. The world that he writes of is likened to 'Jerry Springer with a break beat'. He's described as 'outrageously talented. Eminem has a verbal dexterity, wild imagination and quick-fire delivery beyond the scope of most of his rapping contemporaries'. Andrew Motion, the Poet Laureate, reviewed his collected lyrics in a broadsheet newspaper.

He writes songs in which he's killing his mother and his former wife. George Bush called him 'the most dangerous threat to American children since polio'. Dido says that he's 'totally charming . . . a genius, he's witty and funny but people confuse his character with his songs'. He narrowly escaped a jail sentence for carrying a concealed weapon in a nightclub, a charge to which he pleaded guilty in exchange for the dropping of a charge for assault with an unloaded gun. The night before this incident he was arrested for waving a gun at the friend of a rival rapper.

Confused about what he's really like? To borrow a phrase, 'Will the real Slim Shady please stand up?'

Whether you know him as Marshall Mathers, Slim Shady or Eminem (the name is a play on his initials and his favourite sweets), there's no escaping him. He has outsold everyone, a white rapper in a predominantly black genre, and enjoying heavy rotation on seemingly every music video channel there is.

What would Jesus say to Eminem? It might tax your imagination even to consider the possibility of such a meeting. Even to those of us who know that Jesus was a man who went out of his way to be with people who didn't seem in the slightest bit religious, it takes some imagining. Yet it's bound to be exactly what Jesus would do.

Watch your mouth, boy!

Some people, in taking a guess at what Jesus would choose to talk

to Eminem about, would home in on the lyrics that he delivers.
After all, as has been observed, we live in strange times when rap
artists, 'up on stage, adopt the requisite, rolling lavatory-squat and
heap vile and menacing abuse on the people who have paid to
watch [them]'.[4] Wouldn't Jesus tell Eminem to watch his language?

 A record that contains more swearing than you'd get from
Graham Taylor on the touchlines at an England international.[5]

The Bible certainly has strong things to say to us about the
devastating effects of the words we speak. Writing 2,000 years
before rap, James writes to the early church:

> . . . the tongue is a small thing, but what enormous damage it can do. A
> tiny spark can set a great forest on fire. And the tongue is a flame of
> fire. It is full of wickedness that can ruin your whole life. It can turn the
> entire course of your life into a blazing flame of destruction, for it is set
> on fire by hell itself.[6]

It's lethal! The tongue is a small part of the body but it exercises
a great deal of influence over how we live. A spark from it can
inflame any situation, causing terrible devastation. It makes great
boasts, it lies, insults, swears, gossips, exaggerates and misleads.
Consider the vast swathes of devastation caused during the Great
Fire of London, all starting from a small fire in a baker's shop.

Whoever said, 'Sticks and stones can break my bones but
words can never hurt me', was either lying or stupid. Most of us
can vividly remember some of the words spoken against or about
us, and indeed can call them to mind at any time. Some of us have
been wounded, permanently scarred, by words directed at us. As
well as wounding others, we can do ourselves a lot of damage
from the way we use our tongues, too. There's a warning here:
the tongue can corrupt the whole person, setting the whole course
of our lives on fire.

Not only is it deadly; it's impossible to tame. 'People can tame all kinds of animals and birds and reptiles and fish, but no one can tame the tongue. It is an uncontrollable evil, full of deadly poison.'[7]

This is an incredibly serious warning about the words that we speak and how we speak them. And although our first reaction might be to protest that this is an exaggeration, on second thoughts we can all recall things we wish we had never said and wish we could take back. While it's possible to exercise a degree of control over what we say, none of us can exercise perfect control over the way we use our tongue because the tongue is ultimately untamable.

Actually, there was one person who was able to control his tongue, and not only his own, but also the tongues of others. He met a deaf and dumb man and healed him. The cure for this man's ears and tongue was so dramatic that the crowds who saw it exclaimed, 'Everything he does is wonderful. He even heals those who are deaf and mute.'[8] Another man was famed throughout his region for crying out throughout the day. The Bible describes him as out of his mind and in terrible torment, possessed by demons. After an encounter with Jesus he was restored, sitting quietly and in his right mind.[9] Only Jesus seems to have this kind of power. Many of us can vouch for the fact that we were changed after Jesus stepped into our lives in a powerful way. We're nowhere near perfect, but we're changed and continuing to change.

Eminem is evil (but read on)

It might surprise you, but I don't think Jesus would make a big fuss about the swearing or hateful words that spill from Eminem, whether they are bile or a clever postmodern analysis of American society. You see, in talking about this subject it would be the easiest thing in the world to point the finger at Eminem for the way he uses his tongue. But he can't help it. You see, he's evil. That sounds very judgmental of me, but I'm just quoting Jesus. He had strong words of his own to say about the tongue, but rather than simply picking on profanities, Jesus went to the heart of the matter.

'No good tree bears bad fruit, nor does a bad tree bear good fruit. Each tree is recognized by its own fruit. People do not pick figs from thorn-bushes, or grapes from briers. The good man brings good things out of the good stored up in his heart, and the evil man brings evil things out of the evil stored up in his heart. For out of the overflow of his heart his mouth speaks.'[10]

Jesus says here that we are, of course, constantly revealing the state of our hearts by our words (as well as by our actions). And it isn't always pretty!

You may have noticed that what you think tends to pop out of your mouth. You open your mouth before engaging your brain and often regret the consequences. You see it with children who haven't worked out yet that you don't always say what you are thinking. If you've watched Jim Carey in *Liar, Liar* you'll know what I'm talking about. His son makes a birthday wish that his dad would stop telling lies. And it comes true. For twenty-four hours his dad cannot help but tell the truth. He can't help telling people what he's really thinking. Being unable to tell a lie for twenty-four hours might cause a lot of us problems. It's worse in this case: Dad is a lawyer!

We show the true state of our hearts from the way we speak. Sometimes we show our better side and good things fall from our lips. At other times our words are a painful reminder of the evil in our hearts. We say things in the heat of the moment that reveal that we aren't as nice as we'd like people to think we are, or as pleasant as we like to think ourselves to be. In teaching the crowds who came to hear him, Jesus impressed this fact upon them:

'Listen and understand. What goes into a man's mouth does not make him "unclean," but what comes out of his mouth, that is what makes him "unclean."'[11]

This was controversial because it stood in opposition to the religious thinking of the day, which set rules about what you could and couldn't eat, how you had to wash beforehand, and even the utensils you could use. Jesus' teaching was so alien that Peter had no idea what he meant by it. As a result, we can know with certainty:

> Then Peter asked Jesus, 'Explain what you meant when you said people aren't defiled by what they eat.' 'Don't you understand?' Jesus asked him. 'Anything you eat passes through the stomach and then goes out of the body. But evil words come from an evil heart and defile the person who says them. For from the heart come evil thoughts, murder, adultery, all other sexual immorality, theft, lying, and slander. These are what defile you. Eating with unwashed hands could never defile you and make you unacceptable to God!'[12]

Jesus tells us that the problem isn't the tongue. The words are just the symptoms. As someone once put it, the heart of the problem is the problem of the heart. And as some of those things spill out on to our lips, we're made all too aware of what we're like.

A letter that Paul wrote to the church in Ephesus echoes this:

> Do not let any unwholesome talk come out of your mouths, but only what is helpful for building others up according to their needs, that it may benefit those who listen.[13]

Do you see the problem? It's so much more than simply not swearing. If it said, 'Stop swearing and be polite', it would still be tough for some of us, though we just might be able to manage it. But it goes much further than that. It says, 'Don't be unwholesome – so don't swear, don't put people down, don't speak with bitterness, don't rage, don't slander, don't speak with malice, don't mock, don't make people look stupid by what you say.'

So forget Eminem for a while; who of us is entirely innocent on this score? If these foolish words of ours indicate what is in our hearts, we're all in trouble. Even those of us without the power of speech still have these thoughts in our hearts!

'I just say whatever I want, to whoever I want, whenever I want, wherever I want, however I want.'[14]

It might even be that Eminem would agree with that analysis, at least in part. His career is all about self-expression; his music is predominantly about his life and (in general) how much it stinks. When you then find you sell 30 million albums (and rising), you realize there are a lot of other people out there with the same problem. I'm older than Moby, dismissed by Eminem for being too old to understand his music, so what do I know? But it seems to me that some of the lyrics seem to stray into bad taste. Songs about killing your ex-wife, or your mum with your five-year-old daughter helping (she also sings in the chorus), are pretty sick and shocking. Moby got away lightly! If this is all about self-expression, clearly these things are coming from inside Eminem, just like Jesus says they do for all of us.

 Fame hit me like a ton of bricks. I just got caught up in the drinking and the drugs and fighting and wilding out and doing dumb things.[15]

It's all the rage

Eminem has come to the fore at a time when we all seem to be more and more angry and seem much more prepared to express that rage. Eminem has taken anger and turned it into a fairly dubious art form.

A survey carried out in 2001 by the BBC found that we're becoming an angrier nation. One in ten Britons admit to losing their temper at least once a day and complain that even the smallest provocations cause them to fly off the handle. One in six of us said that we considered resorting to physical violence. Young people under twenty-four were the most likely to lose their temper, the very age group that are most into Eminem's music. No wonder so many identify with his rage.

(One report of this survey commented: 'To their surprise,

however, the section of society with the shortest tempers are parents of school age children, a quarter of whom admit to losing their cool at least once a day.' This leads me to suspect that the researchers had no children themselves!)

What would Jesus say to Eminem? I think he might talk to him about his anger. There are a number of passages in the Bible that talk about anger; it's very realistic about us as people. A letter to the church in Colosse warns the congregation: 'But now you must rid yourselves of all such things as these: anger, rage, malice, slander and filthy language from your lips.'[16]

This reflects what Jesus says about bad language. In essence the problem isn't just the words than come out; it's the problem of the heart. Rage and anger are the problem.

The church in Ephesians is cautioned: ' "In your anger do not sin": Do not let the sun go down while you are still angry.'[17]

See what I mean about the Bible being very realistic about us? It doesn't tell us not to become angry without telling us how to deal with anger when we experience it. Don't forget that these words were written to a church. Again, the Bible shows a complete grasp of human nature, inside and outside of the church. There will be times when we get mad!

James writes to tell Christians: 'My dear brothers and sisters, be quick to listen, slow to speak, and slow to get angry. Your anger can never make things right in God's sight.'[18]

Don't think that Jesus would dwell on the language Eminem uses or even on the subject of the anger itself. I can't see Jesus giving Eminem a warning, an affirming pep talk, and then packing him off to an anger management class, somehow! Jesus would talk to him about something even more powerful than anger, something that would calm that rage. But it's also something that would probably be the end of Eminem as we know him.

Forgive us, as we forgive those who ...
I think Jesus would want to talk about an alternative to anger: forgiveness. After all, it was the very heart of his message,

forgiveness from God and the chance of a new start. That message of forgiveness involves forgiving others. That's an incredibly difficult thing to do. Please don't think I'm underestimating that. Some of us have been badly wronged and the pain from that is still very raw. Yet, even if only for our own sake, we need to get to a place where we are able to forgive.

You see, anger and forgiveness are alternatives to each other. In any situation in which you are wronged you can choose how to respond. You might choose to respond in anger or you might choose to try to forgive. Eminem has plenty to be angry about, and who is to say that you or I, in his position, wouldn't be angry too? He didn't have a great start in life, born to a fifteen-year-old girl who must have struggled to bring him up, especially when young Marshall was abandoned by his father as a six-month-old baby. Home was a series of trailer parks before the family settled in a rough neighbourhood in Detroit. Life didn't give him too much in the way of a head start, and the subsequent all-too-public rows with his mother and his ex-wife confirm that life hasn't been plain sailing, even with all the money in the bank that he now has.

Rapping gave him a way out of working in burger bars and into a form of self-expression that he could never have dreamed would lead him to be so successful. Indeed, his first album flopped, but once he hooked up with Dr Dre (formerly with NWA and producer of Snoop Doggy Dogg) he had the chance and the attention that made all the difference to his career. An almost unique phenomenon as a white rapper (Dre compared seeing him perform for the first time to seeing a black country and western singer), he went on to sell more CDs than any rap artist before him has ever managed. Success has brought plaudits and lawsuits in unequal measure. By the time of *The Eminem Show*, his third (successful) album, America's most dangerous had become America's most wanted. Being such a success, he was soon being taken into the hearts and minds of the very culture he was attacking, just like Elvis, Cliff, Jagger, Bowie, Ozzy Osbourne and all the other one-time rebels.

Eminem's problem is that it's the chaos he lives in that is his muse as an artist. Without a crisis of some sort to be angry about, what is going to fuel his writing? Presumably there are only so many songs expressing hatred for women and gays that you can record before a nation yawns and retunes its sets.

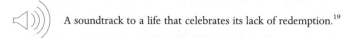 A soundtrack to a life that celebrates its lack of redemption.[19]

We may not know all the hurt that Eminem feels as a result of his dysfunctional life, or the pain that his relationships with his mother and wife, and his lack of relationship with his father, have caused him. (The astute listener will have picked up that there are issues there!) But Eminem can choose what to do about that. He can hang on to his anger and play with it over and over again in his mind and in his lyrics, and grow into a bitter and twisted old man. You encounter people like that, don't you? People who cannot forgive someone something from the past will (apparently) happily tell you, 'I can never forgive them for what they did to me.' It's a free country and it's a choice we can make. In many ways it's the easiest choice to make because we can carry on as we are. There's no need to make the huge and difficult effort to change.

By contrast, we could have a go at forgiveness. Not easy, but surely worth a try? Learning the trick of forgiveness will require strenuous efforts and may never be accepted by the person on the other side of the conflict. But there's a chance to put things behind us and move on. Otherwise, whose life gets screwed up by their bitterness? Often, nobody's but our own.

So I think Jesus would go to the very heart of the matter with Eminem. Forget the cussing and the hatred in the songs: are you going to lose that anger? And how are you going to lose it? Do you want to carry it with you and rave to the grave? Or are you going to try something else, the kind of forgiveness that brings peace and a stable basis for bringing up your daughter?

The danger is that Eminem will carry on writing fuelled by his anger, even stoking it in order to keep the words flowing. This seems to be confirmed by an interview he gave in August 2003, when he admitted,

I haven't had more than a two-day break. Even if I take a break, I'll start writing and I can't control my thoughts. I wanna take a break and then I get angry. I get frustrated if I get writer's block. That's my worst fear – I'll wake up tomorrow and won't be able to write. If there's no drama and negativity in my life, all my songs will be really wack and boring or something.[20]

Sounds like he's angry if he is writing and angry if he isn't – not a good recipe for living. With stakes that high, discovering some way out of this destructive cycle has to be attractive. Finding some peace and stability sounds like a lifeline in a situation like that.

Of course, no-one is pretending that forgiveness is easy. It's relatively easy to forgive someone once, only to find those feelings of anger and resentment returning all too soon. This may well happen many times.

In an exchange with one of his closest friends, Jesus sets us a tough standard. Peter, like many of us, seems to have found this whole business of forgiveness easier in theory than in practice:

Then Peter came to him and asked, 'Lord, how often should I forgive someone who sins against me? Seven times?' 'No!' Jesus replied, 'seventy times seven!'[21]

The consensus among the teachers of the time was, 'Three strikes and you're out.' A brother might be forgiven a repeated sin three times; on the fourth, there was no forgiveness. So Peter is going some here. He reckons that seven times is pretty generous. It's twice what is expected, with one more time thrown in for good measure.

Goodness knows what Peter thought of the response thrown back at him. 'Not seven times; try seventy times that.' And 490 is clearly not a magic number that we are meant to slavishly adhere to; it's saying, 'Just keep on forgiving.' Forgiveness isn't the easy option! Countless Christians have found that it's easier to forgive someone if you've experienced the freedom of being forgiven yourself. Each time that anger or resentment comes back to the surface, we need to practise forgiveness. It'll be hard, but it's that or be eaten up with anger for ever.

Some of us have a slight advantage over others in this business of forgiving people, though we still struggle to do the right thing at times. As people who have experienced at first hand what it is like to be forgiven by God for all the stupid things we've thought, said and done, Christians should be a little better at forgiving others. In fact, knowing the debt of gratitude we each owe for having our slates wiped clean, it's our duty to forgive others. If Eminem were to know what it was like to be forgiven on such a grand scale, he'd find it easier than he expected to forgive.

One final thought. To be serious about forgiveness might well spell the end of his career. Although songs like 'Stan' give a glimpse of something more to his repertoire than out-and-out rage, if it's the anger that keeps him churning out the songs and skits, what happens to him if he loses that anger? If he finds a semblance of peace in his life, will it make his art less exciting? Quite possibly. And even if he finds he is able to keep churning out the songs, there's no guarantee that songs expressing some sort of balance in his life are going to go down well with a generation of disaffected youth. Make no mistake about it, finding peace in his life might be the end of Eminem as a successful recording artist. But then what good is it for a man to gain the world and lose his soul in the process?

6

What would Jesus say 2: Harry Potter?

Quite honestly, I was appalled when I saw the film. The world-wide advertising campaign ensured that children everywhere knew it was coming out. It was, of course, so popular that when it was released clips were often shown on children's television. There was much for people to object to about the film. There was the central part that witchcraft played in it. Adults were teaching young children to use spells and dabble in the occult. There was the bad language, which I didn't recall being in the book.

Sure, there were the amazing special effects, flying on broom-sticks and the exciting sports scenes part way through, but I regretted watching the film with my children. It was too long, and I hate films where characters break into song for no apparent reason. Given the chance to watch *Bedknobs and Broomsticks* again, I would politely decline the offer.

Bedknobs and Broomsticks was released in 1971. Whether it provoked the kind of concern that Harry Potter has I can't remember. When I saw it as a child I wasn't really aware of that sort of thing. I do know that I didn't ever aspire to become a wizard as a result of seeing the programme. I still had ambitions on the football pitch in those days.

I don't start this chapter this way to poke fun at those responsible parents who decide, after a great deal of thought, that they don't want their children to see Harry Potter films or read Harry Potter books. I just want to point out that there's nothing new on the earth, just as the writer of Ecclesiastes frequently reminds us in the Old Testament. The same old things raise their heads, and each new generation has to work out what, if anything, to do in response.

The concern over the Harry Potter books is very real and heartfelt. Some, concerned by the central part the books give to magic and witchcraft and spells, feel they are a dangerous initiation into a dark world. Today, a lot of media output aimed at children seems to promote witchcraft and associated ideas. From *Mona the Vampire* to *Sabrina the Teenage Witch* and *Buffy the Vampire Slayer*, there's plenty of children's viewing on offer based around the world of witches, wizards and the like. Perhaps more worryingly, there are plenty of articles in magazines aimed at young girls that print cut-out-and-keep 'spells' and include articles on how to read palms.

Curiously, board games, computer games, cartoons and teen-magazine articles on these themes (not to mention Philip Pullman!) attract less concern than the Harry Potter books. Perhaps it's simply that the books are brilliantly written, and as a result sell like hot cakes. It has been calculated that every seven seconds someone starts to read a Harry Potter book. I'd be surprised if the vast majority don't finish the book, and in turn all the others in the series. In June 2003 it was reported that the first four books had sold nearly 200 million copies worldwide and that they have been translated into fifty-five languages. Apparently only the Bible has been translated into more.[1] Speaking in October 2002, the chairman of the Frankfurt Book Fair opened the event by saying, 'The industry depends on two young men: Jesus Christ on the one hand and Harry Potter on the other.'[2] It seems that in the search for meaning after September the Eleventh, only Jesus and books about him could begin to touch the Potter phenomenon. And all this is before you add in the phenomenon of *Harry Potter and the Order of the Phoenix*.

J. K. Rowling originally wrote the books for nine-to-twelve-year-olds, although they have become such a craze that lots of younger and older children and adults have read them. The first of the books, *Harry Potter and the Philosopher's Stone*, was voted the best children's book of all time in a survey of children and a parallel survey of adults. *Harry Potter and the Goblet of Fire* came second and *Harry Potter and the Chamber of Secrets* third.[3] It says something about my taste that I prefer *Harry Potter and the Prisoner of Azkaban*.

Somehow the publicity and excitement surrounding the publication of *Harry Potter and the Order of the Phoenix* managed to surpass that of the previous books, with fans queuing to be first in line when the tills opened at midnight in thousands of shops. The Post Office had to lay on extra vans to cope with the demand for the book, each volume 766 pages long and weighing a kilogram. It may have been longer than the New Testament, but that didn't stop a lot of people finishing it the same weekend it came out. There's no doubt that Harry is a literary phenomenon all over the world. The theft of a lorry-load of the books, days before publication, prompted headlines around the world as well as the rather hopeful plea from the police that anyone offered the book before the publication date should refuse it.

The story of J. K. Rowling's rise from writing in coffee shops to being higher on the rich list than the Queen is well known. It was reported that sales of *Order of the Phoenix* on the first day alone netted the author over £10 million. In an interview she did with Jeremy Paxman, J. K. Rowling claimed not to know how much she was earning, or even how much she earned in the previous year. Refusing to be drawn on her true worth, she did say, 'I met my accountant recently and I said: "They say in the rich list that I am richer than the Queen, so that means that you've embezzled quite a lot of money ... I certainly have not got £280 million." '[4]

On top of that came the small matter of the merchandising and the films. The first film made $980 million. That's all. One day Potter-mania must run out of steam, but at the moment *Harry Potter and the Audience of Apathy* seems a long way off.

> There are Hogwarts castles for £79.99, a £100-a-piece Hogwarts Express train set, a Harry Potter Polyjuice Potion Maker, a Harry Potter Weasley family 'Flying Car', a Harry Potter Slime Chamber Playset, a Harry Potter trivia game, as well as the usual DVDs, computer games, chocolates and sweets, including Bertie Bott's Strange Flavour Beans in tomato, horseradish and carrot flavours.[5]

For some people, particularly those with religious convictions, Harry Potter is seen as dangerous and something to keep the children away from. Others can't wait for the next episode to come out. Harry is like that, bringing division wherever he goes.

So what do we do with young Harry Potter? The books are all about witches and wizards; the books are magic. Should we avoid them because of that? Or do we happily read them, figuring they are basically a brilliantly written variation on the boarding-school adventures many of us read in our youth, with some magic thrown in for good measure? *Mallory Towers* with broomsticks? One thing is certain, we can't ignore it. It's out there and impossible to escape.

As with the furore over *The Simpsons*, some Christians have come to the conclusion that Harry Potter is a good thing, a way of connecting people to the often neglected spiritual side of their lives. Harry has been championed by Churches Together in England as helping to 'illuminate themes such as the battle between good and evil. The children's books ask people to look again at the selfish material world and the presence within it of Christian values – truth, love and, supremely, self-giving and sacrifice.'[6] The Archbishop of York courted controversy by declaring that Harry Potter and *The Lord of the Rings* are more spiritual than much Church of England worship.[7]

On the other side of the controversy, there are parents who are concerned about the prominent and positive portrayal of witchcraft in the books and are understandably concerned that the books could be an unhealthy influence on young minds.

What would Jesus say to Harry Potter? I think there are two main things that he'd have to say to the Harry Potter phenomenon, one quite negative and one positive.

Let's start by thinking about some of the negatives about Harry Potter. I think Jesus would have a warning for anyone who seriously thought going to Hogwarts would be a good idea.

Warnings against witchcraft

Some of the critics of all things Harry Potter have taken things to ridiculous extremes, sometimes missing the point completely. Among those criticisms are that brooms and pointed hats are phallic symbols and that therefore the books are evil, or that Harry's lightning-flash scar is an evil symbol because it is half of the swastika.

The thought that J. K. Rowling is somehow promoting Facism is ridiculous. If some of the critics were less blinkered, they'd surely recognize that one of the features of the second book is a thinly veiled attack on racism. The Aryan-looking Draco Malfoy is almost portrayed as a shining advert for Hitler Youth in the films. (Interestingly, 'Malfoy' is a play on the French for 'bad faith'.) In the second film Malfoy is all for ridding the school of mudbloods, those born with some muggle (non-magic) blood in them. The battle for racial purity is firmly lost, thanks to Harry and his friends – one of the many examples of a positive moral message in the books.

There are plenty of other examples of this in the books, as well as a willingness to engage in thinking about the bigger questions of life. In the fifth book, for instance, an exchange between Harry and Professor Dumbledore touches on the inevitability of suffering for human beings. Dumbledore tells him, ' "Harry, suffering like this proves you are still a man! This pain is a part of being human – " "THEN – I – DON'T – WANT – TO – BE – HUMAN!" Harry roared ... '[8]

Some people, however, are concerned by the central role that the books give to magic and witchcraft and spells, and feel they are a dangerous initiation into a dark world. In the United States some of the outcry has been generated by parents who are frustrated with what they see as the promotion of witchcraft (a recognized religion) in a culture where prayer is not allowed in schools.

One result of all the media interest in magic is that youth workers have reported an increased interest in the occult and in children dabbling with casting spells and the like in schools. I'm told by the youth worker in my own church that these things are a problem in our local secondary schools. In particular, there's a great interest in good and bad magic, a world that mirrors, among many others, that of Harry Potter.

If, as is feared, Harry Potter tempts any of us or our children into occult practices, we have every reason to be concerned about it. The last thing any responsible adult wants to do is encourage anything that will lead their child towards a life of witchcraft.

Carol Rockwood, headteacher at a Church of England primary school in Chatham, banned the books from the school library. Her reasoning was that the Bible taught 'that wizards, devils and demons exist and are real and dangerous, and God's people are told to have nothing to do with them'.[9]

She's right; the Bible does contain stark warnings about such things:

> ... never sacrifice your son or daughter as a burnt offering. And do not let your people practice fortune-telling or sorcery, or allow them to interpret omens, or engage in witchcraft, or cast spells, or function as

mediums or psychics, or call forth the spirits of the dead. Anyone who does these things is an object of horror and disgust to the LORD ... You must be blameless before the LORD your God.[10]

The Bible is very clear on this. Witchcraft places you in direct opposition to God and his ways. It's not good to put your faith in these things. They are the wrong things to base your life upon.

I think this is the first thing Jesus would have to say about Harry Potter. He'd want to warn us not to confuse the fiction with the fact. Most children quickly develop an awareness of what is real and what is fiction, though, so talking through the books with your children would be a good idea. Jesus would warn us, 'Don't be stupid and start playing with real witchcraft.' Your mates might be messing about with tarot cards and Ouija boards, but don't touch them. The Bible doesn't warn against it for no reason. Witchcraft comes with a health warning, which is why the Bible says, 'Don't do it.' And notice there's no distinction made here between good and bad magic or between white witches and black magic. The Bible tells us not to get involved in witchcraft, in whatever form – full stop.

I appreciate that for some I'm on controversial ground here. Many people swear by their horoscopes or their tarot readings. They are very firmly in the mainstream these days, with most towns and cities boasting shops that specialize in magic and the occult. A visit to any mainstream bookseller will show you that the Religion or Spiritual section is dominated by books on a wide range of spiritual subjects. Oh, and somewhere in there you'll find some books on the world's major religions, including some books on Christianity.

Presumably this is because people are on the lookout for answers to the big questions of life and for some security in an insecure world. I understand why people want to know something of what the future holds and end up consulting the playing-cards or the dead for some comfort.

The consequences of our actions are always so complicated, so diverse, that predicting the future is a very difficult business indeed.[11]

Professor Dumbledore, no great fan of astrology

The problem with placing your faith in all this is that it's false hope. God warns us not to settle for so little. Don't settle for false hope; don't place your faith in astrology or witchcraft or reading your tea-leaves. It's a waste of time looking to magic rather than to the all-powerful God. When looking for guidance, why consult the dead about the living? One of the things God warns his rescued people about in the Old Testament is not to be sucked into living in the same way as those around them, who don't know what it is to be rescued. Neither do they know the Rescuer.

In other words, don't simply follow the customs of those around you, who live in ignorance of the love of God. Instead, place your trust in God and the provision that he's made for your life.

Now, it is worth mentioning that those who choose to live their lives practising magic or according to their star charts are only following a variation of the pattern of most people in the world. We might be tempted to put those who are into the occult in a special category of evil, because it's mysterious and scary. In his letter to the church in Galatia, Paul warns against the acts of our sinful nature and among them he lists witchcraft – along with envy and jealousy and the rest.[12] Interestingly, in his letter Paul seems to link 'idolatry and witchcraft', and I wonder if this isn't at the heart of the problem.

I have no sense that God is part of the worldview of the Harry Potter books. You could make a case for Dumbledore being a God-like figure in some respects, but I don't think you can push it too far. You could say that Harry's idolatry lies in the fact that he trusts in Dumbledore and magic to help him out of tight situations. That's what Harry puts his faith in. He lives in a world with no obvious reference to God, and so he looks for something else or someone else to place his trust in – as do many of us.

If the thing you devote your time and energies to, the thing that defines you and that ultimately you put your faith in, is not the God who created you and loves you, you're guilty of idolatry too. Not surprisingly, God finds that offensive. But perhaps God is just as offended by other forms of idolatry that take his people away from him. The problem is much wider than witchcraft. Some of these forms of idolatry are so inoffensive in our eyes that we might think nothing of them. Your family, your career, your music, your love life, your car, your garden, your football team, your position in the church, the books of J. K. Rowling – all of these can become the most important things in your life. If they do, they become idols, because they are not God. They are not even close, and yet they occupy the spot that rightfully belongs to him and him alone.

That's the warning I think Jesus would issue to Harry Potter, as well as to those who read the books, watch the films and have the teeshirt. As Jesus said, we need to be single-minded in our devotion to the one God: 'Love the Lord your God with all your heart and with all your soul and with all your mind and with all your strength.'[13]

Idolatry is the business of putting anything else in the place that we should have reserved for God in our lives. We should always have God as number one, followed by whatever else we might deem to be important. The essential problem with witchcraft, it seems to me, is that it's another form of idolatry.

The truth. It is a beautiful and terrible thing, and should therefore be treated with great caution.[14]
Professor Dumbledore to Harry

By her own admission, J. K. Rowling doesn't believe in witchcraft or magic, but understands the fascination that many of us have with stories of wizardry. As a good writer she's done her research into the subject and this has led her into trouble with those who claim that children are being taught the dark arts through her books. This overlooks the instances where she mocks astrology, for instance.

Can anything good come out of Hogwarts?

Is there anything positive that Jesus might say about Harry Potter? I think so. I think he would want to look at some of the themes the books contain. There's plenty to talk about there. Just like us, Harry lives in a moral universe. J. K. Rowling believes that the books are moral, as she told the *Today* show on NBC News, when talking about Lord Voldemort:

> 'I made a very conscious decision right at the beginning that I was writing about someone evil and I wasn't going to tell a lie. I wasn't going to pretend that an evil person is a cardboard cut-out and no-one really gets hurt. If you're writing about evil I think that you have a genuine responsibility to show what that means. And that's why I'm writing them the way that I'm writing them. Actually I think they are very moral books.'

As Philip Pullman points out, there has been a big switch in the nature of books recently. These days many of the successful adult books deal with trivial matters: 'Will my football team win the cup?' 'Does my bum look big in this?' 'My girlfriend has left me and whatever shall I do?' At the same time, children's books are asking 'ultimate questions: where do we come from, what's the ultimate nature of being a human being, what must I do to be good?' [15]

In the books, Harry makes choices about good and bad. Most of the time he's good. Sometimes he's bad. And so he mirrors each of us. As J. K. Rowling says, 'He's every boy but with a twist.'

Here's an example of one of the good choices that he makes. In *Harry Potter and the Goblet of Fire*, Harry is one of four champions involved in a competition. Each champion has to rescue his hostage, and his hostage only, within the hour. If they go past the hour they lose their friends for ever. Harry breaks the rules in order to make sure that all the hostages are rescued. Some have criticized this, saying that Harry encourages children to break rules and be rewarded for it. I would have thought that such actions were to be applauded, but Pharisees throughout the ages tend to see these things differently – something Jesus would surely be able to identify with.

There are plenty of positive things to be said about the books. It could be that Jesus would want to discuss the evil Lord Voldemort. J. K. Rowling describes him fantastically: was there ever a better description of pure evil? Jesus might talk to Harry about Azkaban and the dementors that guard it. They are described this way: 'they drain peace, hope and happiness out of any human who comes too close to them ... get too near a dementor and every good feeling, every happy memory will be sucked out of you. You'll be left with nothing but the worst experiences of your life.' As someone who walked the earth and knew what it was like to be fully human, Jesus might talk about them as an experience of misery that seems to be a lot like hell. Given that he had a sense of humour, he might even joke that the dementors are like some people he'd met!

I think that Jesus would most of all want to talk about scenes towards the end of the first book. As the action comes to its climax, Harry, Ron and Hermione have to pass through a series of trials in order to save the day. One of these is wizard chess. Wizard chess is just like ordinary chess, except that the pieces are alive and take great delight in violently disposing of the pieces they line up against. But this is no 'ordinary' game of wizard chess, because the three of them are involved in a life-sized game, with each of them taking the place of a piece. Ron Weasley, who knows a thing or two about the game, directs the forces for the black pieces:

> Their first shock came when their other knight was taken. The white queen smashed him to the floor and dragged him off the board, where he lay quite still, face down.
>
> 'Had to let that happen,' said Ron, looking shaken. 'Leaves you free to take that bishop. Hermione, go on.'

Every time one of their men was lost, the white pieces showed no mercy. Soon there was a huddle of limp black players slumped along the wall. Twice, Ron only just noticed in time that Harry and Hermione were in danger. He himself darted around the board taking almost as many white pieces as they had lost black ones.

'We're nearly there,' he muttered suddenly. 'Let me think – let me think . . .'

The white queen turned her blank face towards him.

'Yes . . .' said Ron softly, 'it's the only way . . . I've got to be taken.'

'NO!' Harry and Hermione shouted.

'That's chess!' snapped Ron. 'You've got to make some sacrifices! I take one step forward and she'll take me – that leaves you free to checkmate the king, Harry!' . . .

'Ready?' Ron called, his face pale but determined. 'Here I go – now, don't hang around once you've won.'

He stepped forward and the white queen pounced. She struck Ron hard around the head with her stone arm and he crashed to the floor – Hermione screamed but stayed on her square – the white queen dragged Ron to one side . . .

'What if he's – ?'

'He'll be all right', said Harry, trying to convince himself.[16]

Ron does an amazing thing here. He's prepared to sacrifice himself for the good of his friend. How many of us would be prepared to do that? If I were about to be smashed around the head by an enemy, how many of my readers would be prepared to take my place? Would you put yourself between me and my assailant, taking the full force of the blow?

It's possible that someone would do that for me; a friend might – but I doubt it.

I think Jesus would point out to Harry Potter fans something very obvious and yet incredibly profound. I think he'd draw a parallel between Harry's world and that of the Bible. These words are written by the apostle Paul; they are some of the most powerful in the Bible:

> You see, at just the right time, when we were still powerless, Christ
> died for the ungodly. Very rarely will anyone die for a righteous man,
> though for a good man someone might possibly dare to die. But God
> demonstrates his own love for us in this: While we were still sinners,
> Christ died for us.[17]

Christianity is a rescue religion, with Christ the rescuer and you
and me the rescued. We were powerless and in deep trouble.
Unlike Harry, we couldn't wave a wand and make the problem
disappear. Our problem in the face of evil is that we are – partly at
least – evil people. We may not be Voldemort, but we've all done
things that, if we were at Hogwarts, we wouldn't want Dumbledore to find out about.

As we've said a number of times (and you're probably sick to
death of being told), in the language of the Bible we're sinners.
Through the things we've done, said and thought we've acted as
rebels against God and his ways. As rebels we're God's enemies.
It's important that we understand that. Each one of us – there are
no exceptions – has rebelled against God. That rebellion makes us
God's enemies. We may not want to admit it to anyone else, but
we've hardly lived up to our own standards for life, let alone
God's.

Once we understand that, we see that those words of Paul's are
incredibly powerful: 'Very rarely will anyone die for a righteous
man, though for a good man someone might possibly dare to die.
But God demonstrates his own love for us in this: While we were
still sinners, Christ died for us.'

Ron isn't called upon to lay down his life, though we're not
sure whether he knows this when he acts as he does. But he shows
his love for Harry in that he's prepared to sacrifice himself to save
him. For a good man (and Harry is generally a good lad) someone
might possibly dare to die.

But this is how much God loves us: while we were sinners,
while we were rebels and enemies of God, Christ died for us.
Some of us hated God. Many of us didn't give a stuff for him.

Others were ignorant about him or followed him half-heartedly. 'While we were still sinners, Christ died for us.'

Now the question is, would Ron have gone through all that for *Malfoy*? Would he have taken the blow for him? Would any of us go through that for an enemy?

Perhaps you might do that for a friend, but surely never for an enemy. Look at the contrast: 'God demonstrates his own love for us in this: While we were still sinners, Christ died for us.'

We find a similar idea at the end of *Harry Potter and the Order of the Phoenix*. Professor Dumbledore reveals that Voldemort under-estimates the ancient magic that protects Harry: 'I am speaking, of course, of the fact that your mother died to save you. She gave you a lingering protection that he never expected, a protection that flows in your veins to this day. I put my trust, therefore, in your mother's blood.'[18]

This idea of being able to trust in the blood of another is exactly what we find in the Bible. There we read that it was one of the last things on Jesus' mind before he went to his death on the cross. At the last meal he shared with his closest friends they drank wine together. This was to be a meal like no other. Towards the end of it Jesus did something that must have baffled his friends:

> He took a cup of wine and gave thanks to God for it. He gave it to them [his disciples] and said, 'Each of you drink from it, for this is my blood, which seals the covenant between God and his people. It is poured out to forgive the sins of many.'[19]

In the light of the events that were to unfold over the following few days, the disciples would come to understand much more clearly what this meant. The covenant (or agreement) between God and his people was this: the blood that Jesus would shed on the cross, symbolized here by the wine they drank, would cover the sins of many.

This is the Christian message, that Jesus made it possible for each one of us to be rescued. Sometimes Christians speak of trusting in the blood that was shed on the cross. They don't mean this in any mystical way; it's simply a poetic manner of saying that they trust in Christ's death and resurrection for their forgiveness by God, rather than hoping that they can somehow work at being good enough themselves.

Christianity is a rescue religion. Do you want to be rescued? God has done everything necessary for you to be rescued. Christ died for sinners; his death on the cross marks the punishment that we deserved but that Jesus took for us. Because of the cross we can be rescued. All we have to do is admit that we need rescuing, ask God to rescue us and thank him.

It's up to you, a choice that only you can make. And as Dumbledore tells Harry in the second book: 'It is our own choices, Harry, that show what we truly are, far more than our abilities.' [20]

7

What would Jesus say 2: David Beckham?

The joy of Becks

He and his wife Victoria attract huge media attention wherever they go. It's commonly said that in the aftermath of the Charles and Diana saga Posh and Becks have become the couple that fill the gap in the tabloid pages and the nation's consciousness: a new royal couple, no less. In a world of hype and spin, headlines proclaiming that there had been an attempt to kidnap one of them might be readily dismissed as a bizarre publicity stunt. Not so with the Beckhams; they simply don't need the publicity. It might have sounded like a more unlikely storyline from *Roy of the Rovers*, but it turned out to be all too real.

David Beckham OBE is a cult figure and a marketing dream. He has appeal across the spectrum. You may not even like football, but there's still a good chance that you love Beckham. The England captain stares down at you from billboards, and every new look is splashed across the press for style commentators to pore over. A new tattoo: what can it mean? A new haircut, and thousands have copied it by the weekend. A new fashion: wearing a sarong! Well, even David is entitled to the occasional mistake. Sometimes he's on the back pages too, scoring an outrageous goal from the halfway line, running the Greeks ragged single-handedly, or scoring within 126 seconds of his league debut for Real Madrid. His appeal is strong and seemingly universal, whether to young girls, their mothers or his famed gay following. Beloved of football fans, style writers and sociologists, he's an icon. Transcending mere personality he has become a brand. One of the reported reasons Real Madrid signed him was the strength of his brand in Asia, a market the club had yet to crack. Real's marketing director, José Angel Sánchez, described Beckham as 'a massive merchandising machine, worth about £90 million'. He takes a useful free-kick, too.

He's an icon in pretty much the whole world. We saw the hysteria that surrounded his every move in Japan during the World Cup Finals. You may have read about the Buddhist monks who quite literally made an idol of him, creating their own statue of him. Only in the football (sorry, soccer)-resistant USA is he a relative unknown; the Beckhams' appearance on the Stateside ABC net-work in 2003, together with the growing success there of the film *Bend It Like Beckham*, might indicate that the couple have an eye on an unconquered territory.

Fan Mari Kobayashi said at the airport, 'He is just so much more exciting to watch than Japanese players. He is gorgeous.'[1]
Beckham-mania in Tokyo, where nine out of ten people know his name

Fame has always been an ambition for the pair. Victoria recalls, 'I wanted to be one of the kids from *Fame*. I just wanted to be famous. I wanted to be a dancer. Then I wanted to be a singer.' David agrees, 'I have always dreamed of playing for Manchester United and being famous and being a famous footballer.' As easily the most famous couple in Britain, they've made it!

To think that it all started for David with kicking a football! Sometimes, in all the hype that surrounds him, it's easy to forget that David Beckham kicks a bag of wind around a field for a living. But how! Some churlishly moan that he doesn't tackle much or go past many players, but when you work that hard and pass the ball that well, where's the need?

What would Jesus have to say to David Beckham? He seemingly has everything in life: worldwide fame, an abundance of skill, good looks, a pop-star wife, and, according to the 2003 *Sunday Times* Rich List, a fortune of some £50 million, a great deal of this coming from the endorsement deals he has signed. What would Jesus have to say to him?

I think there is a lot that Jesus would say that was very positive about Becks. He's a man who takes being a good father and husband very seriously, which, coming out of the culture of 'the new lad' (very much in vogue at the start of his career), is a marked difference from some of those around him. Victoria recalls noticing that while his teammates headed straight for the bar at the end of a game, Beckham spent time with his mother instead. This marked him out as different and got her attention. In his (first!) autobiography David has a chapter entitled 'My First Team'. This chapter doesn't talk about all the great players he has played with and against, but about his family. Lest we be in any doubt about the importance of his family to him, see what he writes in his second autobiography:

> When Romeo was first lifted up into the light of the operating theatre, the feelings of excitement and happiness, of pride and awe, just flooded through me with all the same intensity they had three years before when Brooklyn was born ... It took my breath away how much I loved Victoria right there and then, how much I loved our brand new baby son ...
>
> I like the feeling that those boys are with me, even when I'm away from home. And not just in my heart. I had their name tattooed on my back after each one was born. There's a guardian angel there, too, looking after them both.[2]

David knows that he's a role model for a whole generation and takes the responsibility of that very seriously. If you were looking for a role model, you could do an awful lot worse than choose David Beckham. Despite being such a massive talent, he's incredibly modest and seems to be unbelievably down to earth given all the attention that he gets every day.

Is it all about what you look like?

Beckham's fame is self-fulfilling now. You get big articles about Beckham, and then big articles about why there are big articles about Beckham.[3]
Jon Holmes, sports agent

Here's a slightly bizarre question. For all his global fame, what do we really know about Beckham the man? For someone so in the limelight, not a lot. As with virtually all footballers, we don't know much about his political or religious opinions, or his views on pretty much anything. We know he liked the film *Taxi Driver* because it inspired one of his more outlandish haircuts, but despite all the photo shoots and all the column inches written about him, we don't actually know much about him as a person. What we do learn from the publicity machine tends to be tightly controlled, and as a result we end up knowing little of substance.

Even with the publication of *My Story*, the 400-page auto-biography, we didn't learn a whole lot more about David. We had confirmation that he had his run-ins with Sir Alex, that he loves his wife and children and that he's an all-round top bloke. There wasn't a lot that was new there, although, given his general diplomatic stance whenever faced with controversy, we did at least have his opinions on a few matters. Other than the revelation that he was so low at one stage that he actually considered walking away from the game, it was a fairly typical footballer's autobiography, though it didn't tell us a great deal that we didn't already know.

Ellis Cashmore, Professor of Culture, Media and Sport at Staffordshire University, argues that it is this that helps to give

Beckham the profile he has. Because his interviews seem tightly regulated, he doesn't give much away about anything of any consequence. As Cashmore comments: 'This may make him appear a blank page; but, of course, anything can be written on a blank page. There are as many Beckham texts as there are readers. It's the very absence of definitive content in the text that makes it so gratifying. Fans can read into Beckham whatever they want.'[4]

As if to prove this thesis, in April 2003 we were treated to the extraordinary experience of a film-maker trying to persuade us that, because Beckham is so well dressed, into the right music and completely cool, he is in fact black! You doubt whether fans can read into Beckham whatever they want? You didn't watch *Black Like Beckham*.[5]

So, despite our fascination with Beckham, we know far more about his image than we do about what he's really like as a person – which means we can make up whatever we want about him to suit ourselves. A result of this is that his following consists of Buddhist monks, gays, people with no interest in football, mums, young children, followers of fashion and even the odd footie fan! With such a wide appeal, he's a marketer's dream.

Even further than this, though, as such a blank canvas with tremendous talent, a pop-star wife and great wealth, he represents our ambitions, our dreams, our aspirations. He has been described as an advertisement for a life that doesn't exist.

I hope I've made clear that Beckham is a great footballer. I have no doubts about that. Yet this is about more than being one of the best players on the planet. If he was ugly with it, or playing for a lesser club, or less dedicated, or more outspoken, he wouldn't be the icon he is today. As it is, everything comes together to make Beckham an extremely high-profile and powerful icon. It's far from being all about image – he's a brilliant footballer – but image plays a massive part. After all, if he looked like Peter Beardsley, David Beckham wouldn't be where he is today.

And that whole issue of image is a very powerful thing to us. No wonder so many of us would change places if we could. Who wouldn't want to be like Beckham? I don't know about you, but I have an image problem. I was never meant to look like this. Somewhere or other there's a more likely version, the me that I was always supposed to be, the me I carry around in my head rather than the me that jumps out from the bathroom mirror. I'm the wrong shape: bits of me are too big, bits of me are too small, and bits of me are just plain in the wrong place.

Meanwhile I see a world of TV shows and advertising where the fit and fashionable hang out and have a great time. It's a fantasy world, where I get to see the wedding photos of Posh and Becks because a magazine figures it's worth £1 million to have the rights to publish them. It's a world where ordinary kids get to ride their bikes and hang out with Beckham. We live in a world where the brand is the key to the kingdom. Wear the right clothes and the world is your oyster, you're part of the club, you're in with the in-crowd. You may not actually get to party with David Beckham, of course, but by fitting in you shouldn't end up getting kicked until you wet yourself in the playground (for example).

What would Jesus have to say about this? I have to confess that the Bible doesn't talk much about image. Jesus and the disciples didn't have a Max Clifford figure in the background spinning their story and giving them PR advice. Given that Jesus lived in a very different world from ours, isn't this one of those areas where Jesus would have nothing to say to us?

BECKHAM, rightly or wrongly, is now the biggest thing in Britain. He has achieved, according to advertising experts, 100% UK household recognition.[6]

Actually, I don't think so. I think Jesus would take the chance to talk about something that at first may seem to have nothing to do with image: character. You see, the Bible isn't too interested in what we look like; it's more interested in what we *are* like. Character is much more important than image.

To illustrate this, Jesus might tell him an old story from the life of David, the great Old Testament king of Israel. The background to this story is that the old king, a man called Saul, had gone bad. So, guided by God, Samuel was sent to find a new king. Look what happened when God was searching for a new king to rule over Israel for him. Who did he pick? An impressive-looking man? In Jesse and his sons he had a family full of them to choose from, yet this is what happened when Samuel went shopping in search of a king:

> When they arrived, Samuel took one look at [Jesse's son] Eliab and thought, 'Surely this is the LORD's anointed!' But the LORD said to Samuel, 'Don't judge by his appearance or height, for I have rejected him. The LORD doesn't make decisions the way you do! People judge by outward appearance, but the LORD looks at a person's thoughts and intentions.'[7]

Jesse's sons were strapping, good-looking guys. Samuel took one look at Eliab and reckoned it was mission accomplished. It was a no-brainer. The others were good candidates, but this was obviously the one. Samuel had one hand on his flask to anoint him with the oil that would signify that he was the next king, when God told him to hold back. This wasn't the one. He looked like the best candidate; but it wasn't about image, it was about character: 'People judge by outward appearance, but the LORD looks at a person's thoughts and intentions.'[8]

Jesse nudged another son and Abinadab stepped forward. He strutted his stuff in front of Samuel, but 'Nope' was the verdict. How about Shammah, then? No. This one? No. That one? No. And so it went on. Jesse had brought his seven sons to audition for the part of king and each of them ended up stamped 'Reject'. Presumably Samuel was a bit perplexed by this point. 'The Lord has not chosen any of these,' he told a disappointed Jesse. 'Are these all the sons you have?'

Jesse then told him about his youngest son David. He had been left behind to work while the rest of the family went to the ball.

The others might be about to celebrate and sacrifice to the Lord, but the sheep needed to be looked after, so they left him at home. I guess they figured that he was the least important, the least likely to succeed. So they didn't even bother bringing him. He was a good-looking lad, but he wasn't the big guy that his brothers were.

He was sent for. When Samuel saw him, guided by God, he said, 'He's the one.'

Why? Because 'The LORD does not look at the things man looks at. Man looks at the outward appearance, but the LORD looks at the heart.'[9]

Or, to put it another way, character is much more important than image. It's one thing to look good. It's quite another to be good, isn't it? If we devote more time to looking good rather than to trying to be good, we make a dumb choice. Who are we trying to fool? The people around us might fall for it, but there's no kidding God. It's one thing to look the part, but quite another to be the man or woman that you should be.

God's priority is what we are like on the inside, not what we look like on the outside. Looking around, that's a good thing. Looking in the mirror, that's a good thing. Imagine if God was interested only in a church of glamorous and fit men and women! If the test of whether we'd go to heaven depended on how we looked in a swimsuit, Becks and Posh might be all right, but most of us would be going to hell.

Is it all about what you do?

To be fair, I am sure that David Beckham knows that character is more important than image. This is why he practises so hard to hone his skills rather than spend more time at the hairdressers'.

His diligence in training paid off when he needed to step up to take a free-kick against Real Madrid for Man Utd in the Champions League. As he takes up the story,

We got a free-kick on the edge of the Real penalty area, just to the right of the 'D'. If I'd been picking and choosing, I might have wanted to be a yard or two further out. The closer you are to goal the quicker you need to get the ball up and then down again to beat both the wall and the keeper. This one looked like a tricky 50 pence worth to me: from this range and against this opposition. I'd practised it tens of thousands of times on my own, on a training pitch – Wadham Lodge, the Cliff, La Baule, Bisham Abbey, Carrington – after everyone else had gone home. Teaching my foot, my leg, the rest of my body how it felt when I got it right ... It's the spot on your boot and the angle at which it meets the ball. Step up. Strike. All the practice leaves you knowing, instinctively, when one's on its way.[10]

It's his discipline in training, carrying on after everyone else has showered and gone home, that shows that David knows that character is more important than image. We saw more of his character after that famous red card.

It's hard to believe now, but there was a time when Beckham was public enemy number one in English football. After kicking out at an opponent in a World Cup game against Argentina in 1998, he was sent off and roundly blamed for England losing the game. In response, tabloid newspapers burned his effigy and printed a darts board with his face as the bull's-eye to give out to readers. Radio phone-ins asked, 'Should David Beckham ever be forgiven?', and polls showed that the public thought it was a very close call. It got to the stage where David and Victoria had to have police protection.

His reaction to all this was to win the fans back by showing tremendous mettle in buckling down and letting his skills on the pitch do the talking. At each away ground the following season he was the target of quite horrible vitriol against himself and his family. With very few exceptions (after all, he isn't perfect), he has shown himself to be above reacting to that kind of provocation. Even David Beckham needs some forgiveness for the mistakes he's made in his life, and perhaps going through all he did after the 1998 World Cup makes it easier for him to understand that.

Unlike some of the greats of sport he seems determined to get the very most out of his career. He's well known for training longer and harder than most of his colleagues, staying behind to take free kick after free kick, determined to perfect his art.

This attitude of making the best of his gifts is something to be saluted. Jesus told a parable about a boss who entrusted varying numbers of talents to three different people. It describes the kingdom of heaven:

> 'Again, it will be like a man going on a journey, who called his servants and entrusted his property to them. To one he gave five talents of money, to another two talents, and to another one talent, each according to his ability. Then he went on his journey. The man who had received the five talents went at once and put his money to work and gained five more. So also, the one with the two talents gained two more. But the man who had received the one talent went off, dug a hole in the ground and hid his master's money.'[11]

Make no mistake about this: talents are very precious. Historically, a talent was the largest unit of weight, around 30 kg, and it was used for gold, silver and other precious metals. Writer John Ortberg has done the maths and reckons that in this context a talent was the equivalent of about fifteen years' wages! (We're talking about the average wage rather than the £90,000 per week that Becks is said to be earning at Real Madrid, but, all the same, it's a great deal of cash.) The boss in the story entrusts one talent to one of the individuals, two to another and five talents (worth seventy-five years' wages!) to a third.

Having been given these talents, the servants are then left to get on with it and make the best of them. You don't have to be Mastermind to work out that the parable is about the way God gives us talents and expects us to do something with them. As with all of us, and very obviously in his case, Beckham has God-given talents. Don't forget that this parable is about the kingdom of God, so the main point is that people are given talents by God to play a part in building that kingdom. But there's a wider point that we might get from this: that we need to make the very best of what we are given. No-one could accuse David Beckham of burying his talents. While others, such as George Best and Paul Gascoigne, are widely judged not to have made the most of their extraordinary talents, Beckham has worked hard at being the best that he can be. One of the challenges Jesus might issue concerns what we do with those talents and whether we acknowledge that they come from a generous God.

Is it all about what you earn?

 In addition to his salary of around £90,000 a week, Beckham is estimated to earn approximately £17 million a year from endorsements.[12]

Beckham is a brilliant footballer. But he's much more than that. He's an icon, partly because he played for so long for one of the biggest sports teams anywhere in the world, Manchester United. This is not unimportant. He added a great deal to the Man Utd brand and at the same time Man Utd gained a great deal from having him as a player, both on and off the pitch. You could argue that Beckham wouldn't be the same iconic figure if he didn't play for one of the very top teams, which is why it had to be Real Madrid when he did finally move. He's a glamour player playing for glamour clubs, and as each new million-pound endorsement rolls in he's reaping the rewards.

With great success has come great reward, and Jesus may well talk to the Beckhams about that. Though we might prefer it to be otherwise – why does he keep going on about it? – Jesus had a great deal to say about money. Essentially, wealth comes with a health warning. He warned us that if we are devoted to money we can't, at the same time, serve God wholeheartedly: 'No servant can serve two masters. Either he will hate the one and love the other, or he will be devoted to the one and despise the other. You cannot serve both God and Money.'[13]

As Jesus reflected after a conversation with a rich man who was put off by the challenge he heard concerning what he did with his wallet: 'I tell you the truth, it is hard for a rich man to enter the kingdom of heaven. Again I tell you, it is easier for a camel to go through the eye of a needle than for a rich man to enter the kingdom of God.'[14]

It's clearly not easy (though not impossible, as Jesus goes on to make clear) for those of us who are rich to enter the kingdom of heaven: not because Jesus has it in for the rich, but because we can be all too easily blinded to the important things in life if we spend all our time thinking about what we can spend.

It seems that great success can act as a major barrier to working out the truly important things in life. Now, you don't get the impression that Becks is driven by money, though he is canny enough to exploit his talent to fantastic financial effect. (He even lists his sponsors in an appendix to his autobiography!) There is great danger to being wealthy, though. If we are keen to keep what we have at all costs, such an attitude carries a terrible price tag. This is a warning to each of us, even if it will take us several lifetimes to earn a year's-worth of Beckham's wage. Whether we consider ourselves rich, poor or somewhere in between, every single one of us can fall into the trap of thinking more about our portfolio (or lack of one) than we do about God.

In the busyness of increasing our worth, or trying to maintain what we already have, we all too easily push into the background the need to take time to think about the key issues of life. Perhaps we don't even think about thinking about God. Or perhaps we figure we can do that later in life when we are less busy. It's a danger that faces each of us, whatever our situation. David is honest about his unformed views about spiritual things, and the birth of Brooklyn seems to have provoked some thought on the matter. As he records in his autobiography: 'I'm not religious,' he says, 'I don't go to church or pray, but I have a sense of spirituality and I definitely want Brooklyn to be christened . . . I'm not sure if I believe in life after death, I haven't made my mind up yet.'[15]

The sense of spirituality, the sense of some kind of other, the sense of wonder, seems to be universal, cutting across all cultures. Having cried for joy at the news that Victoria was pregnant for the first time, Becks was blown away at the miracle of new birth when Brooklyn and Romeo were born. David is firmly with the majority of us when he says he has a sense of spirituality but is essentially unsure what to do with it. I'm sure Jesus would invite David to look at him. So many in this position, of believing in something but not knowing what, write off Jesus Christ without even looking at him. They have a vague feeling, perhaps, that he was a good man, a teacher, and that he is said to have done some miracles. But, come on! No-one believes that stuff any more, do they?

Those who got a closer look at him certainly did. The disciples came to the realization that this was the Son of God. It was something that they articulated a number of times. In the opening chapter of his biography of Jesus, John writes, 'No-one has ever seen God. But his only Son, who is himself God, is near to the Father's heart; he has told us about him.'[16] The challenge to each of us is to check out those claims for ourselves and not just take from those around us the received wisdom that there's nothing to the Christian faith. When I was in my early twenties I took this challenge and it turned my life upside down. No regrets whatsoever.

Is it all about what you're like inside?
So Jesus might speak to David and Victoria about the dangers that their wealth poses for them. He'd certainly challenge them to look into the business of who he is for themselves. I think Jesus would also want to talk about the incredible phenomenon that Beckham has become. His position as an idol to so many all over the world has to be something that the two would discuss.

Maybe Jesus would talk about the other David again to illustrate this. The shepherd boy David who became king turned out to be a tremendous success in so many ways. But, like the sheep that he used to look after, he went astray. With nothing better to do one evening, he saw from his rooftop a woman in the bath. To cut a long story short (you can read it in 2 Samuel 11) David ended up sleeping with the woman and ordering measures that would lead to the death of her husband. Once someone pointed out to him the error of his ways he had the good sense to confess his guilt to God. We know of David's response because he wrote Psalm 51 to express it. Here are some lines from it (verses 1–3, 7–10):

Have mercy on me, O God,
because of your unfailing love.

Because of your great compassion,
blot out the stain of my sins.

Wash me clean from my guilt.
Purify me from my sin.

For I recognize my shameful deeds –
they haunt me day and night ...

Purify me from my sins, and I will be clean;
wash me, and I will be whiter than snow ...

Don't keep looking at my sins.
Remove the stain of my guilt.

Create in me a clean heart, O God.
Renew a right spirit within me ...

We know from the account of this episode that God, who saw into David's heart, forgave David. The same God who sees into each of our hearts offers to do the same for us. Outrageous though it might seem, even clean-cut footballers like David Beckham and Gary Lineker are in need of forgiveness, because, good though these guys are, they aren't entirely without fault in every area of their lives. They are human, and as such make a mess of things from time to time. The things they say, do and think don't measure up to how God would like them to be. They are just like you and me. None of us is quite as great as we'd like other people to think we are; we are all guilty of sin. Yet each of us is loved far more than we can imagine by the God who knows us inside out and yet still offers to forgive us.

After France '98, Beckham found out about forgiveness on a national scale. But he had to earn it. Beckham's forgiveness was not unconditional. He buckled down and played out of his skin for his club. In the end, football fans were forced to concede that he was a good guy who deserved another chance. Others are not so blessed. Some players have a torrid time at certain grounds, for far lesser 'crimes'. They might even be former crowd favourites who went to a rival club. Football supporters are a fickle bunch. Turning a hostile crowd into a forgiving one is some trick, and I'm sure that David is pleased that he managed to pull it off. Being forgiven is a good feeling.

Yet it has to be even greater to know the forgiveness of God. It's a forgiveness that only Jesus can offer, as we saw when we looked at the healing of the paralysed man earlier. Jesus' message was that we can all return to God, whether we've lived decent or terrible lives, and each one of us can make a fresh start. All we need to do is cry out to God in the way King David did. In fact, if that's something that you know you need to do, it's not a bad prayer to pray. Forgiveness is at the very heart of the Christian message. You can be sure that Jesus would want to talk to David Beckham about the vital importance of forgiveness, because without it we are all lost.

What would Jesus say 2:
Robbie Williams?

After Take That I was supposed to be Andrew Ridgeley, remember? I think I've proved I'm not.[1]

The lad's done good

Against the all odds he was the one who emerged from the boy band to sell lorryloads of records. We all thought that Gary Barlow would be the one to rise Phoenix-like from the ashes of Take That. But nope, it was Robbie who confounded the critics and emerged to sign the biggest record deal ever offered to a British artist. The fact that you may not know who Gary Barlow is, or hardly remember Take That, just goes to prove the point. While Mark Owen is reduced to trying to regain our attention via *Celebrity Big Brother*, Robbie is the one with the successful career.

While he has yet to break the States, he's a firm favourite with audiences in much of the rest of the world. He has shown the critics a thing or two with the scope of his work, even recording an album of swing favourites and performing them at the Royal Albert Hall. The Brit Awards keep rolling in and he's a staple in the periodic polls that ask us who we love. Perhaps slightly ludicrously, he's even been voted second in the poll to find the best male singer of the millennium, as well as sixth in the list of the most influential musicians of the last thousand years. Not bad, hey?

His success has meant that he carried on living life in the public eye, a trick he learnt as part of Take That. It led to the ups and downs of his relationships as well as his difficulties with alcohol and other drugs being well documented in the papers. A move to Los Angeles and a decision to stop drinking have given him some peace, and it's still so far so good in respect of his career. Late in 2002 Robbie re-signed to EMI for a reported £70 million, although it's said that only £55 million of that is an upfront payment. The rest depends on how successful he is, and he insists the deal 'does not include in any way, shape or form America'.[2]

With the record-buying public at his feet, a reputation for being the heir of Freddie Mercury as a stadium entertainer, and riches beyond his widest dreams, you'd think he'd have it made.

But there are signs that Robbie isn't as happy as he thinks he should be. His success doesn't seem to satisfy him fully. As he admits with engaging self-deprecation, 'I wanna be David Bowie or Iggy Pop and I'm more like Norman Wisdom.'

On tour a vivid and regular picture is painted of him spending most evenings drinking water and playing the children's card game Uno with the members of his entourage who aren't out on the town. Sometimes the pattern is broken when he has a girl brought to his room. For all the adulation, it doesn't strike you as being a very soul-rich way to live. And it's not as if the adulation does a lot for him. He often makes comments that indicate that having thousands of people screaming for you is a hollow experience as far as he is concerned.

In a revealing interview given to Q magazine in August 2003 Robbie revealed that he had come to recognize that cocaine, drink and soulless sex don't suit him and that what he really needs is a wife. He was also candid about his battle with depression. He takes antidepressants and has come to the conclusion that 'I think I am happy because of the pills'. Asked how he would be without the medication, Robbie told how the pills block out internal scalding voices that dog him. 'It would be Good Morning, you are ****! You are a ******! You are a charlatan and they already know that you are a charlatan. Oh, and you know why you haven't got a girlfriend? Because you are socially inept. And that's before I brush me teeth.'

Robbie is not unusual in being on antidepressants; many of us are. Similarly, he is not unusual in finding that being successful and achieving your goals aren't quite as satisfying as you might have imagined. Some of us experience that on a small scale, while others find out that it's just the same with success on a much larger scale. As Robbie noted in an interview given just after the triumph of playing to 375,000 people over three nights at Knebworth, 'I am seriously thinking about giving it all up and not putting out any more records. I'm loaded, I can buy anything I want and everyone thinks I must have such a brilliant life but it's actually horrible.'[3]

If you're being followed 24 hours a day you have no life . . . As soon as you go out flashbulbs are going to go off, which is going to draw attention to you . . . And it's trauma to leave the house . . .'[4]

It's never enough

This business of not being fully satisfied despite global success is such a well-worn path that it's become the stuff of clichés (which isn't to say that it is any less uncomfortable for the individual concerned). There are many examples from the world of music and beyond. Robbie isn't the first to discover it, and because none of us can quite believe it ourselves ('It'd take a lot more than £70 million to make me unhappy'), he won't be the last, either.

Many other singers before him have expressed the same sort of dissatisfaction with the view from the summit. Alanis Morrisette, interviewed in the *New Musical Express*, put it this way:

I was ... thinking that adulation and fame and all of that would give me a sense of self-esteem when, as I quickly came to learn (after having success on a smaller scale in Canada) the opposite was true in fact – that, if you're in that situation and your self-esteem is low to begin with, it only amplifies it.[5]

At the age of twenty-six, Billy Corgan of the Smashing Pumpkins seemed to have the world at his feet, and yet he was honest enough to admit that it wasn't quite doing it for him: 'I've got an album that's just got nominated for a Grammy, sold a million and a half records, I have a home, I'm married, and something is still not right in my head.'

So when Robbie finds that it's still hard to feel satisfied despite his success (and perhaps then feels guilty that he's still not happy after all the good things that he has), he's not alone. It seems it's not unusual.

Curiously, it turns out that you can have too much of a good thing. It seems that a life of having whatever, or indeed whoever, you fancy doesn't do you any good at all. It's an apparently ridiculous situation, but all the power and money and sex and status we can get don't turn out to be very good for us. All these things that so many of us spend our lives chasing, or more passively dreaming about, aren't the real deal.

What would Jesus have to say to Robbie Williams about this? I think he might first point him to a book that he has probably never come across before. It's tucked away in the Old Testament, and most people in the world don't even know it's there; which is a tragedy because it's a book with everything to say to the culture of the western world.

It's called Ecclesiastes, and I'd heartily recommend you to read it. You might need the contents page to find out where it is, but it's well worth turning up. It's written by a man who had had tremendous success in pretty much everything that he'd ever done. Yet it had all left him with a gnawing sense of not having found what he was looking for. Despite his best efforts at seeking pleasure and meaning in life, that true, deep satisfaction was still proving elusive.

The search described in Ecclesiastes is one we all undertake to a certain extent. For some of us it might be fairly half-hearted, but the author of this book was diligent. He applied himself to a great study; he was deliberate and persistent. Since we aren't here for long, he asks, what can we do while we are here that would be worthwhile?

He started by devoting himself to pleasure. After all, in the search for meaning in life there's no point in starting with austerity, is there? Here's how he describes his experiment:

> I said to myself, 'Come now, let's give pleasure a try. Let's look for the "good things" in life.' But I found that this, too, was meaningless. 'It is silly to be laughing all the time,' I said. 'What good does it do to seek only pleasure?' After much thought, I decided to cheer myself with wine. While still seeking wisdom, I clutched at foolishness. In this way, I hoped to experience the only happiness most people find during their brief life in this world.[6]

He's almost scientific in his analysis of his studies. He starts by stating his conclusion, 'Pleasure is meaningless', and then records his methodology: he looked for pleasure and tried laughter, wine, folly.

Yet his conclusions make him sound like a right misery, don't they? Laughter is foolish. Not a guy to invite to your next party, then. Even if you were to invite him, the chances are he wouldn't come. You see, he's partied out. The word used for 'laughter' here is associated with messing about and playing games at parties, with loss of judgment and being completely frivolous – the sort of attitude that says, 'Forget tomorrow, let's party!' It's the kind of partying that exists in its own fantasy bubble, with no regard for the morning. Anything that threatens to break into that bubble is swiftly kept at arm's length. Don't forget he was looking for a meaning to life. He isn't saying you should never ever laugh, but he is saying that if you're looking for meaning in life you won't find it in the Comedy Store.

Wine doesn't work, either. It can be very pleasant to share a bottle with friends. But if you're looking to cheer yourself with wine on a regular basis you know you're on to a loser. I used to work in a hostel for homeless men. Some of the guys there tried to cheer themselves with cans of Special Brew. There was some mad laughter as a result, but absolutely no evidence of joy. The footballer Paul Merson recalls how he was so addicted to drink that he started taking cocaine in order to be able to carry on drinking. He thought it would help him to sober up faster so that he could start all over again. Look at what it did to him!

Laughter and wine are good things. But don't go looking for meaning in them. They are empty. You can be sure that the writer enjoyed himself a fair bit on the way to his conclusions, but at the end of it all he says that if you look to these things for meaning, you'll be disappointed.

He 'clutched at foolishness', too. This is quite simply all about over-indulgence, doing whatever you want, defying wisdom. It's the kind of environment identified by a fashion designer no less than Vivienne Westwood: 'We have no choices, only a terrible turnover of gimmick and nonsense. Everyone tries to keep up with the times; it leads to a mad vacuum.'[7]

So pleasure doesn't seem to do it. Sheryl Crow could have told us that, if we'd chosen to listen rather than just sing along. In lines written from bitter experience, her song 'If It Makes You Happy' asks a poignant question: if something makes us happy it must be OK, so how come we're so sad?[8] As an interview with the *New York Times* in 1999 revealed, 'several of the people Sheryl Crow has written songs with have met tragic ends, including Kevin Gilbert, who died of autoerotic asphyxiation, and John O'Brien, who committed suicide'.

No-one is advocating a 'no fun' policy here. Some Christians seem to view fun as suspicious. I'm certainly not going to suggest that we join them. The writer says here that, if you live a life dedicated simply to living for pleasure, and if you're planning to live a life of self-indulgence – doing what you feel like when you feel like it – you're in trouble.

So the writer of Ecclesiastes decided to do something constructive. He embarked upon a number of great projects. He was a tremendous success at pretty much everything he turned his hand to. How's this for a record of achievement?

> I also tried to find meaning by building huge homes for myself and by planting beautiful vineyards. I made gardens and parks, filling them with all kinds of fruit trees. I built reservoirs to collect the water to irrigate my many flourishing groves. I bought slaves, both men and women, and others were born into my household. I also owned great herds and flocks, more than any of the kings who lived in Jerusalem before me. I collected great sums of silver and gold, the treasure of many kings and provinces. I hired wonderful singers, both men and women, and had many beautiful concubines. I had everything a man could desire! So I became greater than any of the kings who ruled in Jerusalem before me. And with it all, I remained clear-eyed so that I could evaluate all these things.[9]

Not a bad CV, is it? True, he was never part of a fantastically successful boy band and he never won any Brit Awards, but otherwise he seems to have done it all. He undertook great projects, built houses and planted vineyards (kind of unfortunate, as he was later to discover that drinking wine isn't the answer to finding ultimate satisfaction in life!).

He created gardens and parks, planted fruit trees and irrigated his plantations (the timber would have been very valuable in his time and place). His wealth is further underlined by the fact that he had slaves, huge herds and flocks, silver and gold and treasures from around the world. Add to these the singers he owned and the harem, and it seems he didn't lack for much. Some believe the author of this book to be Solomon, a man of great wisdom and wealth. He was also a man with 700 wives and 300 concubines.

(I'm not quite sure where he got his reputation for being wise!) His final assessment: 'I was the greatest – ever.'

In his search for meaning in life and true satisfaction, then, the writer of Ecclesiastes enjoyed great achievements and wealth and power and sex. And still he was not satisfied. You might be beginning to suspect that there was no pleasing him. The thing is, there's a fundamental flaw in his search. I wonder if you've noticed what it is.

It's completely self-centred, isn't it? He's got 'I' trouble. Look at his report: 'I undertook, I built, for myself . . . I made . . . I bought, I owned . . . I amassed for myself, I acquired . . . I became greater by far than anyone.'

When we're searching for meaning, we tend to centre things around ourselves. We have the self at the centre. That was the problem of the writer of Ecclesiastes too. Look at how it continues:

> Anything I wanted, I took. I did not restrain myself from any joy. I even found great pleasure in hard work, an additional reward for all my labors. But as I looked at everything I had worked so hard to accomplish, it was all so meaningless. It was like chasing the wind. There was nothing really worthwhile anywhere.[10]

The writer didn't exercise any self-denial. He took everything he liked the look of; he wasn't one to ever refuse a pleasure. Notice that it wasn't all doom and gloom. There was some satisfaction in all this. He took delight in his work.

Donald Trump has been quoted on what motivates him in business: 'For me the important thing is the getting, not the having.' The writer of Ecclesiastes agrees – there was some satisfaction there; the activity itself was satisfying. Yet when he stood back and saw what he had achieved, what had he gained from all that hard work?

Nothing. It was all meaningless. As he puts it, 'There was nothing really worthwhile anywhere.' This is almost an archetypal sentence from Ecclesiastes. There are phrases that crop up again and again in his writing: 'everything was meaningless', 'it was like chasing after the wind', 'nothing really worthwhile'.

> You don't deserve all this and it's all going to be taken away from you anyway. If it is my lot that this all gets taken away from me then there's something I need to learn from it. But also, if this stays with me for the rest of my life, then there's something I need to learn from that, too.[11]
> *Robbie Williams reflects on his riches and success*

Thinking about it, you really wouldn't want him at your party. He comes across through most of the book as suffering bitter disappointment. His search for meaning is fruitless.

I wonder – do you believe the writer of Ecclesiastes? Most people don't. Look at that list of achievements again. How many of us can honestly say we wouldn't like the inventory at the end of our lives to read like that? If we honestly believed that achievements and wealth weren't where it's at we'd be different people. We wouldn't flog ourselves to death at work. We wouldn't have midlife crises over how little we'd achieved in life, knowing we've only got another few years left on this earth. Most of us admire people who've done well. Robbie Williams is a popular guy; he came seventy-seventh in the poll of the Greatest Britons ever, for heaven's sake! He's achieved things, he proved a sceptical music press wrong and he's rich.

Who of us doesn't privately – in our hearts – drool over the description we read? 'Anything I wanted I took. I did not restrain myself from any pleasure.' Many of us would like to live that way. So Robbie Williams reckons that wealth and fame aren't the be-all and end-all, eh? We might not say so publicly, but a lot of us would like the chance to find out for ourselves. So touring and playing in front of thousands of fans is terrible, huh? Most of us have our doubts. We wonder if perhaps all the rich people haven't got together to propagate the myth that it's terrible lazing around having anything you want all the time.

George Bernard Shaw, hardly the most religious man who ever lived, once wrote that there are two tragedies in life. One is to lose your heart's desire. The other is to gain it.

The ultimate meaning in life, the highest good to which we can give ourselves, is not pleasure. Pleasure promises more than it can produce. Its advertising agency is better than its manufacturing base. In looking for a foundation to build your life upon, don't look to pleasure. It cannot sustain you.

If you live solely for pleasure, for what is immediate and pleasurable, it's little wonder that you won't find any meaning to your life. There seems to be an inherent paradox within hedonism: the more you search for pleasure the less of it you find.

There is this huge devil inside me. And it doesn't come out and act against other people; it just wants me to destroy myself. I have a disease that talks to me in my own voice and tells me I haven't got it. And that's my dark side.[12]

Familiar words – 'I am the way'

The first thing Jesus might do in talking to Robbie Williams, then, is to direct him to this old book. It describes the timeless struggle of men and women through the centuries to create some meaning to their lives. But on the face of it, Ecclesiastes just seems to reinforce the fact that we have a lot of questions and issues to be dissatisfied about. It's all very well telling us we find satisfaction elusive, but we knew that already, thank you very much. How about some answers? In the absence of clear guidance from the writer of Ecclesiastes, where do we go to discover how Robbie, or any of us, can find satisfaction? What would Jesus say to Robbie Williams on this point? I think he'd be likely to reply with some words I know Robbie is familiar with: 'I am the way.'

Jesus first uttered these words to his closest followers when he was trying to get them to see that his death in Jerusalem was only hours away. At the Last Supper Jesus took the last opportunity he had to explain things to his disciples.

John, who was there at the time, records three long chapters'-worth of material concerning this final meal. It must have made some impact on him! One of the things that stands out in all that Jesus told his disciples is this statement: 'I am the way, the truth, and the life.'[13] It's quite some statement!

First of all he provides direction for the lost, saying, 'I am the way.' How do you react when you're lost? Chances are it depends on whether you're male or female. The classic male finds it hard to ask directions. We'd much rather drive around in circles in the hope of stumbling across our destination, assuming, of course, that we are prepared to admit that we are lost at all!

Many of Robbie's lyrics indicate that he might be brave enough to admit to that feeling of being lost. In 'Feel' he sings of having too much life running through his veins and of it going to waste. He says he doesn't want to die, but he isn't all that keen on living either. Then comes the killer punch. In the chorus, he longs to experience real love for ever, but inside him is a big empty space, one that shows on his face.

It's well articulated, that feeling of unfulfilment. What are we here for? Where do we fit in the scheme of things? It's the theme of a great deal of contemporary art. As he sings in *Escapology*'s 'Something Beautiful', your friends may think you have it all, but they can't see deep inside you.

Despite their phenomenal success and any number of sexual encounters, it seems that celebrities who can have anything they want are still in need. Freddie Mercury has been widely quoted as saying, 'You can have everything in the world and still be the loneliest man, and that is the most bitter type of loneliness. Success has brought me world idolization and millions of pounds, but it's prevented me from having the one thing we all need: a loving, ongoing relationship.' As *Friends* star Matthew Perry discovered, 'all your dreams coming true when you are twenty-five is not necessarily the best thing in the world … it's not as fulfilling as I'd hoped'.[14]

Jesus says that the whole point of life is to live in harmony with the Maker, to experience the love of God in an ongoing relationship. Jesus goes even further than that: he says he is the way to a relationship with God. Now if that is truly the point of it all, being right with God through Jesus, it's safe to say that most of us have missed the point of our existence down here.

Bernard Levin, the columnist, is keen to stress most adamantly that he is *not* a Christian. He describes the exact same feeling that Robbie sings about in 'Feel', that feeling of there being a hole inside most of us. Levin describes how we respond to that void:

> Living lives of quiet and at times noisy desperation. Understanding nothing of the fact that there is a hole inside them and however much food and drink they pour into it, however many motor cars and television sets they stuff it with, however many well-balanced children and loyal friends they parade around the edges of it, it aches.

If we're honest, it's not an experience that most of us are unfamiliar with. I believe there are times when we all feel we are missing that indefinable something. We try all sorts of things in that hole, hoping they will fill the gap. St Augustine reckoned there is a God-shaped hole in all our lives and we are never satisfied until we fill it with the only thing that fits. The bold claim Jesus makes is that he is the way to fill that gap.

I wonder what Robbie makes of this bold statement from Jesus? They are familiar enough words to him. 'Jesus in a Camper Van' from the album *I've Been Expecting You* contains the lines:

> I suppose even the Son of God gets it hard sometimes,
> Especially when he goes around saying I am the way.

These lines came back to haunt Robbie and co-writer Guy Chambers when they were successfully sued in 2000 for lifting the lines from an old song. The claim that Jesus makes, to be the way, is even more controversial than we first might imagine. But before we examine that in a little more detail, let's look at those claims to be the truth and life.

The appeal to be the truth is attractive to many of us, living as we do in confusing times. Many of us feel a sense of mild bewilderment from time to time at the world that we live in. I cannot begin to imagine what it must be like to end up remarking to a stadium crowd, 'Have you any idea what it feels like to be stared at by 60,000 people?', and knowing that this is the tip of the iceberg, that those 'mere' 60,000 men and women represent many millions of people who buy his records, hear him on the radio and read all about him in the papers. What on earth does that do to your head? The book *Robbie Williams: Somebody Someday* records the band tiptoeing around the star, and the management making sure that everything he could possibly want is his whenever he wants it. Though it's the dream of many a *Pop Idol* candidate, it's not the greatest way to live. In the circumstances, Robbie seems reasonably well adjusted, writing sarcastic songs in response to being voted the world's most handsome man and mouthing to the camera off-stage, 'I'm not bothered', while the audience sings along with his songs.

 If I wasn't Robbie Williams right now, I'd probably be auditioning for the *Big Brother* household.[15]

Jesus' claim, 'I am the truth', offers us some sanity and reality in a confused world. Again it's a claim as bold as brass. When he makes that claim, Jesus says Christianity (following him) is either true or false. So it doesn't make sense to say, as some do, that 'Christianity is OK for you, but I'll find my own way'.

Jesus either is the truth, as he claims, or he's not. If it's true, we all need to do something about it, unless we're foolish enough to be content to settle for lies and half-truths.

If it's false, I for one am deluded; I've fallen for it. You might have come to that conclusion. If it's true, you've fallen for something else, in which case you're the deluded one. Either way it has to be something of the utmost importance. C. S. Lewis summed it up by saying that if Christianity was false it is of no importance; if it is true it is of great importance. The one thing that it cannot be is of moderate importance.

Neither can Jesus' claim to be 'the life'. Again, it's such a stark claim that you have to decide what to do about it. This wasn't the first time that Jesus' followers had heard him tell them this. On a previous occasion Jesus told them he was the resurrection and the life, and he then proved it by raising an old friend, Lazarus, from the dead.

Here, Jesus repeats this claim again: 'I am the way, the truth, and the life.' And he claims to be able to raise us from the dead too. The Bible talks about us being dead in our sins. Jesus asserts that we can be raised to a new life, free from the guilt of the way we've lived without God.

These claims – to be the way, the truth and the life – are not small. As if these weren't enough food for thought, Jesus makes a further claim that continues to upset millions of people around the globe: 'I am the way and the truth and the life. No-one comes to the Father except through me.'[16]

In other words, no-one gets to God except through Jesus. A relationship with him is the only way to find true satisfaction. If we ignore God and live a life that centres around ourselves, no wonder it feels meaningless – we aren't living in the way we were designed to.

The key to understanding Ecclesiastes is this phrase 'under the sun'. In other words, if you live your life under the sun, as if life in this world is all that there is, don't be surprised if it all feels meaningless. This isn't the way you were created to live. Right from the beginning of the Bible, in Genesis, we read that we were created a certain way for a certain purpose. We were created in God's image, for a relationship with God. Part of that is living the way that God instructs. It's only in relationship to God that you'll find true meaning.

And it might just be that Jesus' claim makes sense to Robbie Williams. As he sings about needing someone to love in the chorus of one of his songs, you wonder whether he knows that it's something more than the love of a good woman that he's looking for. 'Love Somebody' speaks to God like a prayer; Robbie admits to feeling him in the silence and sees the need to let him in. Only love will grant him the freedom he longs for.[17]

The search for happiness is difficult. Could it be that Robbie is on to something?

What would Jesus say 2: Paula Radcliffe?

> The race was not even one-fifth run and her head was bobbing up and down like a crazy horse and her arms pistoning away as if she was auditioning for a Duracell advert.[1]

What an improvement!

It's one of the universally recognized truisms of sport that no-one remembers who came second. Cast your mind back over some sporting events of the past: FA Cup Finals, Olympic races, golf tournaments. Pick a year, and many sports fans are able to tell you who collected the trophy or the winner's medal. But unless you are fanatical about rowing (in which case you should be able to work out which team came second in each University Boat Race), chances are that you'll struggle to name the gallant (and not so gallant) losers in sport. Winners get remembered; losers are quickly forgotten.

There are, of course, exceptions. Some competitors are so quirky that the chances are you'll never forget them. Eddie the Eagle's ski-jumping exploits were famously so far behind the rest that he ended up celebrated for it. The same was true of the record slow performance of swimmer Eric 'the Eel' Moussambani in the 100 metres freestyle of the Sydney Olympics as he represented Equatorial Guinea. But they are very much the exception, memorable only for their mediocrity among world-class athletes.

Other performances are memorable because they are so gutsy. When Paula Radcliffe ran the 10,000 metres in the Sydney Olympics she didn't come second. She didn't even win a medal. Her race plan was to hit the front from the starting-pistol and keep running. It's accepted athletics wisdom to pace your race so that you run within yourself and save something for a big finish. Generally it's at a point somewhere in the last 600 metres or so that you kick off and try to break the other runners left in the race. In Sydney, Paula's tactic was simple. She tried to break as many of the field as she could from her very first stride.

Long before the halfway stage she had reduced the leading pack chasing her to four other runners, two of them Olympic gold medalists and one a world champion. She was clearly setting a pace that only the world's finest athletes could live with, and then only just. They were trailing her at 5,000 metres and they were still in her wake at 7,500 metres. Then, with 2,000 metres remaining, Wami and Tulu of Ethiopia and Ribeiro of Portugal all passed her.

You'd expect all to be lost in that situation, but Paula isn't one to give up so easily. Noticing that they slowed the pace down once they were in control of the race, Paula knew that she must have hurt them and so she came straight back at them. With four laps to go she hit the front again. Another 1,000 metres and Paula had broken the runner in fifth place, Laroupe of Kenya. Now there were four of them chasing three medals with just 600 metres to go.

As the bell sounded for the last lap it was clear that she'd given her best and it wasn't quite enough. The only three who could stay with her swarmed past and it was the girl from Bedford who missed out on a medal. Devastated, despite running faster than she'd ever run before, she faced the press and asked, 'Who remembers who finished fourth?' before breaking down in tears.

I'm sure it's no consolation whatsoever to an athlete of her ambition and drive, but the truth is that many who saw that race will never forget it.

That was at the end of 2000. Her husband and coach, Gary Lough, describes the time as 'the lowest point. Oh, it was hard to sit and watch that happen.'[2]

Fast-forward a few years and the also-ran was World Female Athlete of the Year, BBC Sports Personality of the Year, twice winner of the London Marathon (including the first time she ever ran the distance), a 5,000 metres gold in the Commonwealth Games, a 10,000 metres European record, and a woman who breaks the World Marathon record anytime she feels like it. Oh yes, she was awarded an MBE as well. Her dominance of her sport is such that it was deemed too expensive for organizers of the 2003 London Marathon to take out insurance against her breaking the world record again. They were quoted a premium of 70% of the prize money they would have to pay her, and as it turns out they should have taken the deal.

Although there was the disappointment of missing the 2003 World Championships in Paris through injury and illness, Paula bounced straight back in September by setting a new world record in a 5 km road race, her second competitive race after her injury. She also holds the world records for the marathon and for 10 km. She is an incredible athlete.

What was it that changed her from an also-ran into a world champion? Presumably many factors were involved, but top of the list must come her complete dedication to what she is doing. It's something she has always had. She recalls as a fourteen-year-old being so dedicated to running that she would go to bed at 9pm rather than join her friends at a party because she had a race that week. It was that kind of dedication that saw her qualifying for the World Cross Country Championships at just fifteen years of age. It's also that single-mindedness that saw her get a First in Modern Languages at Loughborough University while continuing her international athletics career.

What would Jesus have to say to Paula Radcliffe? Would he have anything to say to her at all? After all, there's no record that Jesus showed any particular interest in track or field. I think Jesus *would* have things to say to Paula. Believe it or not, the Bible does actually talk a little bit about athletics. First of all, Jesus might talk to Paula about dedication and hard work, and point her to some letters written to the early church.

Dedication's what you need

Paul wrote letters to a church in Corinth. He used images and ideas that his readers could readily identify with. Corinth was well known for, among other things, the Isthmian games, which were staged every two years. They were second only to the Olympics in importance. When Paul wrote to the church and wanted to communicate the importance of living a godly life, he used the image of an athlete in training:

> Remember that in a race everyone runs, but only one person gets the prize. You also must run in such a way that you will win. All athletes practice strict self-control. They do it to win a prize that will fade away, but we do it for an eternal prize. So I run straight to the goal with purpose in every step. I am not like a boxer who misses his punches.[3]

Even those who are uninterested in athletics know that only one of the runners in a race get a prize (unless they are children in schools committed to non-competitive sport!). If you are in training for a serious competition, you don't show up on the day with the vague feeling that perhaps you should have done some training or at least bought some trainers. No, says Paul, you go into strict training beforehand. You make sacrifices and punish your body, pushing yourself ever onwards in order to put in your very best performance on the day. No athlete runs aimlessly; you run with purpose and with a plan.

Paul wrote like that because he was determined to succeed –

not simply to win a race, but to make sure that he was living as he should as a follower and servant of Christ: 'I discipline my body like an athlete, training it to do what it should. Otherwise, I fear that after preaching to others I myself might be disqualified.'[4]

Having preached the message of Christianity to anyone who would listen, the last thing that Paul wanted was to miss out on the prize himself. That would be a disaster! As well as warning others not to miss out on the prize, Paul was adamant that he wanted to finish the race too. So, in order to give it his absolute best, he trained hard.

This is language that any athlete understands. Paula Radcliffe, with her commitment to being the best that she can be, would fully understand this. Paula's training regime in the build-up to a big race is awesome. I'm tired just reading it.

She's unusual among athletes in that she takes a regular day off, training hard for seven days and then having a complete day off. She doesn't conform to the typical picture of an athlete in the way that she trains, either. She understands that, because of everything she puts her body through, she needs plenty of recovery time; so she tends to sleep for eleven hours a night, getting up at around 9am. After her training she'll sleep for a further couple of hours in the afternoon. So far so good. I think that most of us, with a little preparation, could manage sleeping for most of the day.

But that's only $\frac{13}{24}$ths of the story. Paula packs more training into the remaining eleven hours than most of us could manage to fit into a fortnight. She typically runs between twelve and fifteen miles in the morning and winds down with a seven-mile run in the evening. As well as running around 135 miles a week, she has weights sessions and works on her core stability as well. So this business of punishing your body to achieve your very best is familiar enough. She knows all about it. You don't take 1 minute 29 seconds off the world record for the marathon the second time you run it without knowing all about discipline and training. Beginner's luck doesn't come in to it. You plan everything to the finest detail and do your very best. You do whatever is necessary to pursue victory single-mindedly. If that means a ten-minute ice-bath after winning a marathon to cut down on the chance of injury, then, like Paula after the Chicago Marathon 2002, you do it.

It's exactly the kind of effort and hard work that should resonate with Jesus' followers. In talking to Paula, Jesus might well direct her to what he said to a man who asked him which was the most important commandment.

> Jesus replied, 'The most important commandment is this: "Hear, O Israel! The Lord our God is the one and only Lord. And you must love the Lord your God with all your heart, all your soul, all your mind, and all your strength." The second is equally important: "Love your neighbor as yourself." No other commandment is greater than these.'[5]

Having been asked for the most important commandment, Jesus replies with two. Neither is particularly easy! Essentially, Jesus tells the man to love God with everything he's got; all of his heart, all of his soul, all of his mind and all of his strength. We are commanded to be dedicated to God, giving him our all. As if that were not hard enough, we are to love our neighbour as we love ourselves. These are the two great commandments. The one thing that stands out when we're talking about them is that following Christ is to be tackled with the same hard work as the preparation for any race. It requires a tremendous effort.

Playing fair

> There's nothing I really go without. In the days before a major race, I might give up cakes. But I would never stop having chocolate.[6]

If Jesus were to point out to Paula the kind of hard work that you need to put into life with God I'm sure she'd understand it perfectly. It was that dedication that saw her become a top-class athlete. Following on from that, he might decide to talk about the importance of competing on equal terms with everyone else.

Inevitably, faced with such a brilliant set of improvements to her performances in 2002, there are bound to be some who mutter darkly that she must have used drugs to achieve those results. This would seem extremely improbable. Paula's outspoken stance on drugs in sport makes it highly unlikely that EPO or nandrolone has had anything to do with her run of good form.

In the 2001 World Championships in Edmonton, Paula drew the attention of the world to the problem of EPO (the drug that is best known through its abuse in cycling's Tour de France) in her sport. She displayed a simple handwritten message demanding 'EPO cheats out' as she watched from the stands, causing controversy worldwide. The incident was sparked by the re-instatement of Olga Yegerova on a technicality after she had been found to have used EPO, and has left Paula looking over her shoulder. The world of athletics being as it is, it is suspected by some that there could be reprisals. One former athlete was quoted as saying that he feared for her life, and, while that might be an over-reaction, Paula has gone on record as saying that she needs to be even more vigilant now to make sure that her drinks aren't tampered with.

Here is another subject on which Paula would be in agreement with Jesus. In another of the letters that Paul wrote, he says how important it is that followers of Jesus should play by the rules. This time Paul is writing to Timothy, a young church leader, and advising him on some of the attributes that are required of a person who is determined to live as a Christian.

> No-one serving as a soldier gets involved in civilian affairs – he wants to please his commanding officer. Similarly, if anyone competes as an athlete, he does not receive the victor's crown unless he competes according to the rules. The hardworking farmer should be the first to receive a share of the crops.[7]

Paul points out that followers of Jesus must be as single-minded as a soldier who serves in the army. Soldiering doesn't leave you with time to get involved in civilian affairs, not if you want to please the commanding officer. As you train for battle you don't have much time for the leisure activities of Civvy Street. You concentrate on your training as a soldier. It's the same for the farmer. Paul was writing before the days of combine harvesters with searchlights on the front. Farmers worked from dawn till dusk to get the harvest in. Even with all the technology at their disposal today, farmers don't have a lot of spare time. It's hard work, and Christians similarly should be prepared to put their backs into their efforts to follow Christ.

Both these images fit perfectly into the life of an athlete. You need to be single-minded in your focus as well as working hard day after day to achieve your goal.

Sandwiched between these two is this third image of the athlete having to play by the rules if she is to wear the victor's crown. In Paul's day there were strict rules concerning how you trained for a race, never mind how you actually ran in the event. If you didn't follow the rules for training you weren't even allowed to enter the race. I guess it's similar now with all the drugs tests between races as well as at athletics meetings. In the context of writing about the church, Paul seems to address the temptation to cut corners and play by our own rules when we compete. Paul is talking about Christians living as they are instructed to live by Christ if they are to win the race of life.

This might all make it sound as though the Christian life is a grind that you have to put yourself through every day, a celestial plot to make sure we don't enjoy life at all. If that's the picture that you have of living as a follower of Christ, you've been misled somewhere along the way. Inviting people to follow him, Jesus said:

'Come to me, all of you who are weary and carry heavy burdens, and I will give you rest. Take my yoke upon you. Let me teach you, because

I am humble and gentle, and you will find rest for your souls. For my yoke fits perfectly, and the burden I give you is light.'[8]

If you think that an eternal training schedule is the only thing on offer here, be of good heart! There's rest on offer here. Another translation of this passage puts it this way: 'Are you tired? Worn out? Burned out on religion? Come to me. Get away with me and you'll recover your life.'

There is a lightness and great joy to living in relationship with the God who made us for that relationship. There is tremendous freedom in knowing that we are in the right with God. It's all about what Jesus has done, rather than any personal best we might achieve. There is tremendous security in knowing that it's his work that keeps us there rather than anything we can muster. Being a Christian has enriched my life in a way I can nowhere near adequately describe. I cannot imagine life any other way. I recommend it wholeheartedly. It is most definitely not a daily grind. But hear this. It's not always a picnic. There are times when it's a real struggle, and bathing in ice would be a cinch in comparison.

 It's the performances and the training that generate the confidence.[9]

I think Jesus would point this out to Paula Radcliffe and to anyone who was thinking about following him: there are tough times ahead as well as good ones. This might come as something of a surprise. It's not unusual for people to be told that becoming a Christian and living as a follower of Jesus means a natural and pain-free existence. Please do not be conned by easy promises of a stress-free life as a Christian. It certainly didn't seem to be the case for the first disciples! Upon deciding to follow Christ you will get the answer to some of your questions and it will solve some big problems for you, such as what life is truly all about (for a start). But you'll probably end up with a new set of questions.

Besides the joy of the resolved conflict between you and your God, you're likely to have new conflicts with one or two people who don't like the fact that you've taken 'this religious thing' a bit too seriously. Living as a Christian in a world that doesn't applaud you as you run the race isn't easy. It requires single-mindedly listening to your coach rather than getting dragged into civilian affairs. It can be hard work sometimes, and you'll need discipline to stick at it. You'll need to work out how to live differently, by the rules rather than bypassing them. Are you prepared for that? Are you willing to put in the hard graft? To live as a Christian isn't a leisurely fun run, it's a serious undertaking. The same applies to Christians as to any athletes who race for a medal in their particular discipline.

I think Jesus would speak to Paula in terms that affirmed her dedication and sheer hard work in pursuing her sport. I think he'd applaud her single-minded pursuit of her very best in her chosen field and her commitment to doing it honestly, without drugs – relying on her best efforts and her punishing training, while she makes the most of her God-given talents. He would also throw down the challenge that following him wouldn't be the easy option (though I wonder if Paula Radcliffe would know an easy option if it bit her on the nose).

Hitting the right targets

But I don't think that Jesus would leave it there. I think he'd talk to Paula about her goals for her racing and about her goals for the whole of her life as well. There's a third passage in the Bible where Paul (who was clearly an athletics fan) talks about how to live as a Christian in terms of training. He's writing to Timothy again:

> Do not waste time arguing over godless ideas and old wives' tales. Spend your time and energy in training yourself for spiritual fitness. Physical exercise has some value, but spiritual exercise is much more important, for it promises a reward in both this life and the next.[10]

Timothy was living and working in Ephesus, where the church had a problem with rogue preachers who tried to get the Christians to obey a load of rules and regulations that had nothing to do with the Christian faith. Paul characterizes these as myths and old wives' tales, and tells the young minister not to get mixed up in them. Instead, he's to get into training, not so that he can run the false teachers out of town, but in order to be godly. He's to train in order to show by his life that he belongs to God. He's to live the godly kind of life that you would expect from a minister or from any believer.

Physical training has its benefits. If you've ever done any, you'll know the truth of that. Perhaps the first time you tried you found that you could hardly do a thing; you were short of breath almost as soon as you started and you ached for a few days afterwards. But if you stick at it you'll begin to notice some difference. Maybe after some months you'll find that you can lift weights you could never have lifted when you started. You can run further and faster. Let's not get carried away; you'll still be half the speed of Paula Radcliffe. But there's no doubt that the physical training you're doing is of benefit.

Yet physical training is of limited value. Training for godliness, Paul tells Timothy, is of greater value. It'll stand you in good stead for the way you live this life and the life to come. This training is valuable for all eternity.

So the final thing I think Jesus might want to flag up to Paula Radcliffe is this. All this physical effort in training is admirable and of great benefit, but there's a form of training that is more important. It's about preparation for something much bigger than even the Olympics.

From my extremely limited experience of training and running, I know that when you're on a treadmill it's hard to see beyond the numbers that move so slowly on the display telling you of your progress. You focus on them and on the way you run and don't really take a lot of notice of what is going on around you. Perhaps that's why the treadmill is used as a metaphor for the way so many of us live. Whatever we're up to, whether it's running or work or family or whatever, we can become so absorbed in the detail of what we are doing that we forget that there's a much wider perspective to life. It would be tragic to spend the whole of life focused on a detail and miss the main point. Yet it's a common mistake that many of us make.

I think the challenge Jesus would make to Paula is this. Think wider. Look further ahead. Don't just focus on the next race, or the next Olympics, or even what lies ahead when the racing career comes to an end. Think about the big things in life. What's it all about? What about God?

Running can be a good time to mull over some of the things that are going on in your life. It offers a chance to shake things down and think them through. Given that Paula isn't one to shirk a challenge, it could be the start of an adventure even bigger than her amazing athletics career.

What would Jesus say 2: You?

It's a mark of our celebrity-obsessed times that we find it interesting to speculate on what Jesus might say to the great and good (or simply notorious) of our generation. I'm sure we can think of lots of people whom we'd like to imagine having a conversation with Jesus. What would he say to George Bush Jnr? Or Saddam Hussein? Or your particular favourite?

One of the things that marks out Jesus is that he had time for all sorts of people. You didn't have to be an A-list celebrity to get his attention. While we might be interested in thinking about what Jesus might have to say to our favourite celebrity, I wouldn't be at all surprised if Jesus wasn't more interested in saying something to the likes of you and me, people who don't tend to turn heads when we walk down the street.

There's a particular story that Jesus tells that applies to all of us, whoever we are and whatever we might think of him. Here's how he told it:

'Listen! A farmer went out to sow his seed. As he was scattering the seed, some fell along the path, and the birds came and ate it up. Some fell on rocky places, where it did not have much soil. It sprang up quickly, because the soil was shallow. But when the sun came up, the plants were scorched, and they withered because they had no root. Other seed fell among thorns, which grew up and choked the plants, so that they did not bear grain. Still other seed fell on good soil. It came up, grew and produced a crop, multiplying thirty, sixty, or even a hundred times.'

Then Jesus said, 'He who has ears to hear, let him hear.'[1]

It's quite a well-known story, but before we explore it, a word of warning. Or, if you prefer, a personal confession. It's not possible to say with any degree of certainty what Jesus would say to anyone. This book has been made up of a series of my best guesses. I've looked at the kind of people Jesus met and then tried to find some modern-day counterparts. I'm confident Jesus reacted the way he was reported to in each encounter because I believe that the Bible is a trustworthy book. But, as his disciples would be quick to testify, you try to second-guess Jesus at your peril.

You see, Jesus isn't predictable. Put yourself in the place of the crowd who had come out to hear Jesus and you'll get an idea of what I mean. We miss this sometimes because, when we do read the Bible, it's often in little chunks without thinking about how it all fits together. In this case, we know that Jesus had a massive crowd of people coming out to hear him – so many that he had to get into a boat and take to the lake in order to get some space. Why were they there? Well, if you read about the previous events, you'll see that Jesus had been gaining a wide reputation.

It might well be that the main reason people came to him was the amazing power he had as a healer. In Mark's previous chapter Jesus was also down by Lake Galilee in a boat because so many were coming to him in order to be healed. Before that, the crowds were so dense that a group of friends had to dig their way through the roof of the house where Jesus was, so that they could reach this healer. Why? Because just before this Jesus had healed many who had been brought to him suffering from various diseases.

News of the healings he had performed spread like wildfire and the crowds grew and grew.

Another reason he attracted such amazing crowds is that he was such a great storyteller. One of his trademarks was that he told a lot of stories, or parables – little spiritual time-bombs that he primed and then planted in people's minds.

Many of the people who listened to Jesus went away realizing that, far from just listening to a master storyteller, they were hearing the summing up of a judge. The parables hold a mirror up to our lives. They challenge us.

This is why I say it's a dangerous business trying to predict with any certainty what Jesus might say to any of us. I think it's likely that most in the crowd came to see and experience healing. In addition, I'm sure many of the crowd were there expecting to hear informative and authoritative teaching about God.

Look at what they got. It has become known as 'the parable of the sower', though it's probably better described as 'the parable of the soils'. I reckon a large number of the crowd will have walked away without the faintest clue of what Jesus had been talking about. On the face of it, all they seem to have got from Jesus is an unrequested and unwanted lesson about gardening.

For what it's worth, I think Jesus *might* use this parable to talk to you and me. I can't be sure, of course, but it would be appropriate because it describes four different scenarios of how we can react to God. Whoever we are, we fit into one of the scenarios. As we look at this, ask yourself which one you fit into.

The parable of a farmer sowing his seed describes a typical scene. Everyone in the crowd would have either sown seed like this themselves or they'd have seen others do so. They'd have known that any farmer would want to sow right to the edge of his field and maximize his resources. As a result, some of the seed would fall on the path, where it had no chance of germinating. In fact, the birds would come and eat it up.

They'd have recognized the problem of sowing in rocky places, where there wasn't a lot of soil, too, because much of Galilee was like that. This doesn't mean that the soil was full of stone, but that much of the land was typically a thin covering of soil over a bed of rock. The farmer wouldn't have known this while he was sowing, because in this time and place the farmer would first sow the seed and then plough it into the ground. Any seed that ended up in this shallow bed of soil would grow, but wouldn't be able to put down any deep roots – there was no way of getting through the rock. So when the hot weather came along, the plants withered, because they couldn't reach further down in search of the water they needed.

A third type of soil is full of thorns (or thistles as some people translate the passage). I'm not the most experienced of gardeners, but on moving into a house with a garden I realized I at least had to have a go. I quickly found that what grows well in my garden is usually the weeds. Thistles and brambles still grow in my garden, despite my best efforts. Those who heard Jesus would know as well as we do that weeds tend to grow fast, and they choke the plants you do want to grow.

Finally we have the fourth kind of soil, which is rich, full of nutrients, free of weeds and rocks, and basically looking like my next door neighbour's. The seed that falls into that soil produced a good crop, 'multiplying 30, 60, or even 100 times'.

This was the story Jesus told the crowd. They were probably waiting for him to get on with the religious stuff. 'I guess he'll come to that in a minute. After all, we didn't come out here for a story about gardening. He's just warming up. I expect he'll tell us something really important soon.'

Yet Jesus finishes it right there. 'He who has ears to hear, let him hear.'

In other words, 'Go figure.'

What was all that about?!
Most of us have heard this story before, and so we aren't nearly as confused as we would have been if we had followed Jesus down to the lake to hear him teach. When the crowds melted away, the

twelve disciples, and a few others who were curious enough to want to know exactly what it was all about, admitted to their confusion and asked him to explain.

Jesus started by telling them that his story about crop-sowing was in fact the secret of the kingdom of God. This probably made them feel even more stupid than they already did. They'd probably missed that, and who can blame them? So Jesus went on to explain what it was all about: 'Don't you understand this parable? How then will you understand any parable?'[2]

In other words, this is an easy one. This is Course 101 – Elementary Parables. If you don't get this, what chance have you got of understanding any of them?

Thankfully, unlike most of those who heard Jesus at the lakeside, we have the inside track on what the parable means. We don't have to go home perplexed by what we have heard.

'The farmer I talked about is the one who brings God's message to others. The seed that fell on the hard path represents those who hear the message, but then Satan comes at once and takes it away from them. The rocky soil represents those who hear the message and receive it with joy. But like young plants in such soil, their roots don't go very deep. At first they get along fine, but they wilt as soon as they have problems or are persecuted because they believe the word. The thorny ground represents those who hear and accept the Good News, but all too quickly the message is crowded out by the cares of this life, the lure of wealth, and the desire for nice things, so no crop is produced. But the good soil represents those who hear and accept God's message and produce a huge harvest – thirty, sixty, or even a hundred times as much as had been planted.'[3]

Here are the clues to help work it out. The seed is the message about God. So it stands to reason that the farmer is anyone who is sowing God's message, whether it's the minister in a church service, you or me when we chat to someone in our lunch break, or a book like this, which tries to explain God's message.

The message about God is distributed all over the place, but people respond to it in very different ways. That message is for everyone, but not everyone will receive it. The four types of soil represent different types of reactions among people who hear that message.

Some are completely unreceptive; it's like the message has fallen on deaf ears. They might have been there in body when they were told the message about God, but from their lack of reaction you wonder if they've actually been listening at all. Their minds seem so full of other things that they don't give what they've been told any thought at all. Jesus said there are people like this. As soon as they hear the word, Satan swoops down like a bird and gobbles up the seed.

A second type of person hears the word and gets really excited about it. They receive it with joy – for a while. But they don't put down any roots, so when the heat is on they wither and die away. Becoming a Christian costs, and the heat of ridicule or abuse is too much for some because they aren't really established. They've got no roots. There's no depth there.

This is a very real danger for a lot of us. Many of us have no church background, and so if we are to join in with a church on a Sunday we may well get stick from our nearest and dearest.

It's very easy for that seed to go to waste. Jesus warns that 'since they have no root, they last only a short time. When trouble or persecution comes because of the word, they quickly fall away.'[4]

If fear of persecution or trouble is going to hold us back, we're never going to bear fruit, are we?

The third type of person hears the word and it takes root and they start to grow, but then the rest of life crowds in and chokes the life out of your faith. Listen to what Jesus describes as the dangers: 'The thorny ground represents those who hear and accept the Good News, but all too quickly the message is crowded out by the cares of this life, the lure of wealth, and the desire for nice things, so no crop is produced.'

Let's unpack that a little. 'The cares of this life.' Do you have cares or worries? Of course you do. Who doesn't? The question is, 'Are they going to grow up and kill off your faith?'

Then there's what Jesus describes as 'the lure of wealth'. We get so wrapped up in what we have, or what we don't have but want, that it kills off our faith. As Logan Pearsall Smith once observed, 'Those who set out to serve both God and Mammon soon discover that there isn't a God.'[5]

You see, if you are going to respond to God's message, it needs to be the number one thing in your life. Nothing else can come close.

What are some of the things that can come in and choke your faith? Some people get so caught up in their work that that's what strangles the life out of their faith. You know how work is these days: your career takes all your time and energy. The pressure is always on to work longer hours. It's easy for work to take up more and more time, and the things of God get pushed out.

For others, the desire that comes and chokes the word is the desire for another person. You meet that special someone, and God's message doesn't seem nearly as exciting now that there's a more immediately tangible expression of love before you. Perhaps you fall in love with someone who isn't a Christian, or perhaps that person is a committed Christian from your church. All too often the effect is the same: your faith gets crowded out.

For others, it can happen when you start a family. You know how it is. The kids take over. They need looking after. I could list some examples, but if you have children of your own you already know that the list is endless. For some it's the physical effort of the job; for others it's the mental strain, or even the tendency to idolize our little clan. For a whole host of reasons, it's easy for children to come in and do the damage to your faith that is described here.

Job, partner, children – all these are common faith-chokers. And you could add so many other things; it's hardly an exhaustive list. Now don't get me wrong, no-one's saying, 'Don't work; don't go out with someone; don't have kids.' I'd be a hypocrite if I did, because I've done all these things.

I am saying that these things bring both pleasures and pressures. Life gets really busy, and so we need to underline this warning from Jesus. Here it is in slightly different words: 'Still others, like seed sown among thorns, hear the word; but the worries of this life, the deceitfulness of wealth and the desires for other things come in and choke the word, making it unfruitful.'[6]

Have your priorities changed recently? Are your relationship with God and your service of him and of others less important than they used to be?

We all need to search our hearts and ask God to show us if this is a danger for us and, if so, where the danger lies.

The fourth type of person is described in Jesus' last sentence: 'Others, like seed sown on good soil, hear the word, accept it, and produce a crop – thirty, sixty or even a hundred times what was sown.' This happens

- *if* you respond to the message about the kingdom of God
- *if* you determine not to live in fear of what your so-called mates think
- *if* you are prepared to put the kingdom of God before anything else – your job, your loved ones, whatever

Then, Jesus says, you are going to be fruitful. You'll have a harvest, maybe even a hundred times what was sown.

Doesn't the chance to do stuff for God and help bring in this kind of harvest excite you? To see people in heaven because you were faithful to God?

Why settle for promotion or a bigger house? Why should we sell ourselves so short when God has much bigger things in store for us?

Of course, it's when we understand more of the parable that we understand its power. Jesus describes four reactions to the message about God and his rescue of people. Instinctively, we find ourselves identifying with one of those reactions.

Whether we are Christians or sceptics or looking into it for the first time, this parable has something for each of us. It's obvious that this is for any of us who are trying to make up our minds about whether the Christian religion is true and to be trusted or not. If that's you, what is your reaction to this parable and to the message in these pages? Will you put the book down and forget all about it? Will you get excited about the message for a short time but quickly change your mind when you realize it might not be a decision popular with people whose opinions matter to you? Will you get excited about the message until other concerns crowd it out and you suddenly realize one day that your faith has been choked out of you? Or will you respond to the message, give yourself to it unreservedly and, over time, share it with many others?

According to Jesus, these are the four options that people have to weigh up. Which is it to be?

One final thing. Those of us who are familiar with this story tend to think this is only about Christians sowing the seed of the gospel message to people who aren't Christians. But it's wider than that. It's about the response of each of us to the word – the preaching of the message of the kingdom of God. It's about how Christians, too, respond to what we read in the Bible. How do we respond to the challenges we read there? How do we respond to what we hear in church on a Sunday? How do we live as disciples of Jesus? Whether we're Christians or not, there's plenty to challenge us in the parables that Jesus told. So forget about what Jesus would say to your favourite celebrity, be it Cilla Black or Wayne Rooney. What is he saying to you?

Notes

1. Philip Pullman

1 *The South Bank Show*, ITV, broadcast March 2003.

2 Peter Hunt and Millicent Lenz, *Alternative Worlds in Fantasy Fiction* (Continuum, 2001), p. 161.

3 *The South Bank Show*, ITV, broadcast March 2003.

4 *Third Way*, April 2002.

5 Hunt and Lenz, *Alternative Worlds*, p. 134.

6 Parsons and Nicholson, quoted in Hunt and Lenz, *Alternative Worlds*, p. 134.

7 Matthew 7:24–27.

8 Philip Pullman, *The Amber Spyglass* (Scholastic, 2001), p. 431.

9 Pullman, *The Amber Spyglass*, pp. 33–34.

10 Pullman, *The Amber Spyglass*, p. 431.

11 Interview with Roy McCloughry, *Third Way*, 1998.

12 Interview with Susan Roberts, <www.fish.co.uk>.

13 Mark 2:1–4.

14 Mark 2:5.

15 Mark 2:6–7.

16 Mark 2:8–12.

17 John 14:9.

18 Woody Allen, *Esquire*, 1977, quoted in John Stott, *The Contemporary Christian* (IVP, 1992), p. 84.

19 Philip Pullman, *The Northern Lights* (Scholastic, 1998), p. 377.

20 1 Corinthians 15:54b, 55, 57.

21 1 Corinthians 15:14–20, NIV.

22 Pullman, *The Amber Spyglass*, p. 35.

23 Pullman, *The Amber Spyglass*, pp. 309–310.

24 Pullman, *The Amber Spyglass*, p. 336.

25 John 14:1–3.

26 *The South Bank Show*, ITV, broadcast March 2003.
27 *The South Bank Show*, ITV, broadcast March 2003.
28 *Lion and One Unicorn*, vol. 23, no. 1 (1999), p. 124.
29 *The Times*, 18 October 2000, quoted in Hunt and Lenz, *Alternative Worlds*, p. 159.
30 Pullman, *The Amber Spyglass*, p. 464.

2. Big Brother
1 *The Mirror*, 13 June 2003.
2 *Rebels Without a Cause*, Day 17, 07:18. *Big Brother* website.
3 Romans 7:15.
4 Paul McCartney and Michael Jackson, 'Ebony and ivory'.
5 Barbara Ellen, 'Why we are watching Big Brother', *The Observer*, 13 August 2000.
6 Matthew 7:1–5, NIV.
7 Oswald T. Pratt and Scott Dikkers, *You Are Worthless: Depressing Nuggets of Wisdom Sure to Ruin Your Day* (Boxtree, 2000), p. 184.
8 John 3:16–17, NIV.

3. Homer Simpson
1 Tom Carson, 'The Gospel According to Homer', © *Esquire*, 1 July 1999.
2 Mark I. Pinsky, 'The Gospel According to Homer', © *The Orlando Sentinel*, 15 August 1999.
3 Frederica Mathewes-Green, 'Ned Flanders, My Hero', <beliefnet.com>.
4 Matthew 22:1–14.
5 Luke 15:4–10, NIV.
6 Isaiah 64:6.
7 Luke 18:9–13, NIV.
8 Luke 18:14.

4. Anne Robinson

1 Anne Robinson, *Memoirs of an Unfit Mother* (Little, Brown, 2001), p. 3.

2 Robinson, *Memoirs*, p. 16.

3 Robinson, *Memoirs*, p. 197.

4 Robinson, *Memoirs*, p. 197.

5 Robinson, *Memoirs*, p. 111.

6 Robinson, *Memoirs*, p. 158.

7 Romans 3:22–24.

8 Robinson, *Memoirs*, p. 204.

9 Mark 7:21–23.

10 Matthew 5:21–22.

11 Matthew 5:27–28.

12 John 3:16–17.

13 John 4:6–7.

14 John 4:9.

15 The full story is in John 4:1–42.

16 Robinson, *Memoirs*, p. 358.

17 Robinson, *Memoirs*, p. 362.

18 1 Timothy 1:15–16.

5. Eminem

1 Charles Shaar Murray, *The Observer*, 12 May 2002.

2 Zoe Heller, *The Daily Telegraph*, 8 June 2002. To be fair, she concedes that her argument at this point 'is going to sound unbearably poncey'.

3 Casper Llewellen Smith, *The Daily Telegraph*, 23 May 2002.

4 *The Daily Telegraph*, 7 January 2003.

5 Smith, *The Daily Telegraph*, 23 May 2002.

6 James 3:5–6.

7 James 3:7–8.

8 Mark 7:37.

9 Mark 5:1–20 tells the whole story.

10 Luke 6:43–45, NIV.

11 Matthew 15:10–11, NIV.

12 Matthew 15:15–20.

13 Ephesians 4:29, NIV.

14 Quoted in Edward Helmore, 'America's New Favourite Son', *The Observer*, 10 November 2002.

15 *The Times Magazine*, 30 November 2002.

16 Colossians 3:8, NIV.

17 Ephesians 4:26, NIV.

18 James 1:19–20.

19 Burhan Wazir, *The Observer*, 18 June 2000.

20 Interview given to <www.teenmusic.com> on 11 August 2003. My source was found at <www.news24.com/News24/Entertainment/Abroad/0,,2-1225-1234_1400502,00.html>.

21 Matthew 18:21–22.

6. Harry Potter

1 *The Independent*, 18 June 2003.

2 Reuters, 8 October 2002.

3 *The Daily Telegraph*, 22 September 2002.

4 *The Daily Telegraph*, 20 June 2003.

5 John Arlidge, 'Harry Potter and the Crock of Gold', *The Observer*, 8 June 2003.

6 *The Daily Telegraph*, 9 October 2002.

7 *The Daily Telegraph*, 8 July 2002.

8 J. K. Rowling, *Harry Potter and the Order of the Phoenix* (Bloomsbury, 2003), p. 726.

9 *The Daily Telegraph*, 9 September 2002.

10 Deuteronomy 18:10–13.

11 J. K. Rowling, *Harry Potter and the Prisoner of Azkaban* (Bloomsbury, 1999), p. 311.

12 Galatians 5:19–21.

13 Mark 12:30, NIV.

14 J. K. Rowling, *Harry Potter and the Philosopher's Stone* (Bloomsbury, 1997), p. 216.

15 Speaking on the BBC TV programme *Omnibus Special: J. K. Rowling*, broadcast winter 2001.

16 Rowling, *Harry Potter and the Philosopher's Stone*, pp. 205–206.

17 Romans 5:6–8, NIV.

18 Rowling, *Harry Potter and the Order of the Phoenix*, p. 736.

19 Matthew 26:27–28.

20 J. K. Rowling, *Harry Potter and the Chamber of Secrets* (Bloomsbury, 1998), p. 245.

7. David Beckham

1 *The Times*, 18 June 2003.

2 David Beckham with Tom Watt, *My Side* (HarperCollins, 2003), pp. 297–298.

3 *The Sunday Times*, 15 June 2003.

4 Ellis Cashmore, *Beckham* (Polity Press, 2002), p. 157.

5 *Black Like Beckham*, broadcast on Channel Four, 28 April 2003.

6 *The Sunday Times*, 15 June 2003.

7 1 Samuel 16:6–7.

8 1 Samuel 16:7.

9 1 Samuel 16:7, NIV.

10 Beckham, *My Side*, p. 357.

11 Matthew 25:14–17, NIV.

12 *The Sunday Times*, 15 June 2003.

13 Luke 16:13, NIV.

14 Matthew 19:23–24.

15 David Beckham and Dean Freeman, *My World* (Hodder & Stoughton General, 2000), p. 44.

16 John 1:18.

8. Robbie Williams

1 Robbie Williams interviewed in *Q* magazine, August 2003.

2 *Q* magazine, August 2003.

3 Williams interviewed in the *Sun*, 18 August 2003.

4 Robbie Williams and Mark McCrum, *Robbie Williams: Somebody Someday* (Ebury Press, 2001), p. 248.

5 Alanis Morissette, interview in the *New Musical Express*, 4 May 1996.

6 Ecclesiastes 2:1–3.

7 Vivienne Westwood, *The Observer's Life Magazine*, 22 January 1995.

8 'If It Makes You Happy', from the album *Sheryl Crow: Special Edition*.

9 Ecclesiastes 2:4–9.

10 Ecclesiastes 2:10–11.

11 *The Daily Telegraph* magazine, 9 November 2002.

12 Williams and McCrum, *Robbie Williams: Somebody Someday*, p. 111.

13 John 14:6.

14 *The Times* magazine, 19 April 2003.

15 Williams and McCrum, *Robbie Williams: Somebody Someday*, p. 271.

16 John 14:6, NIV.

17 'Love Somebody' from Robbie Williams, *Escapology*.

9. Paula Radcliffe

1 Will Buckley, *The Observer*, 1 October 2000.

2 Rachel Cooke, 'In it for the long run', *The Observer*, 1 December 2002.

3 1 Corinthians 9:24–26.

4 1 Corinthians 9:27.

5 Mark 12:29–31.

6 Quoted in Cooke, 'In it for the long run'.

7 2 Timothy 2:4–6, NIV.

8 Matthew 11:28–30.

9 Paula Radcliffe, quoted on BBC Sport Online, 1 August 2001.

10 1 Timothy 4:7–8.

10. You

1 Mark 4:3–9, NIV.

2 Mark 4:13, NIV.

3 Mark 4:14–20.

4 Mark 4:17, NIV.

5 Logan Pearsall Smith, 'Other people', in *Afterthoughts* (1931), quoted in R. Andrews et al. (eds.), *The Columbia World of Quotations* (New York: Columbia University Press, 1996).

6 Mark 4:18–19, NIV.